What Kind of Style is That?

By

Roy Tokashiki

ISBN: 1-4033-7718-9 (Electronic)
ISBN: 1-4033-7719-7 (Softcover)

This book is printed on acid free paper.

1stBooks - rev. 09/11/02

CONTENTS

INTRODUCTION v
REPRESSED MEMORY 1
INTELLIGENCE TEST 3
SKILLS 9
MEDIOCRE NIHLISM 19
DOMESTIC VIOLENCE & CHILD ABUSE AWARENESS 22
RICKY'S Y2K plus (YOUTH 2 KID) 26
WHISKEY TALKIN' 62
OBLIGATORY CHAPTER 123
NOT AN "A" STUDENT 136
WRAPPED AROUND A TWINKIE 144
SPECIAL APPEARANCES BY YOUR COMMUNITY LEADER 158
THERE'S NO "I" IN LOSER 168
SCARE PEOPLE 209
IMITATION IVORY TOWER 221

INTRODUCTION

His name is Ricky Wang. I don't know if it's his real name. He might have been ashamed of what he was doing with the use of a.k.a. name. He could be doing something that you can't tell your parents about its legality or morality. I just know that I have his journals.

My research into the identity of this person revealed that he went by the name of Ricky Wang during his plate lunch salad days. He was in constant conflict on his road taken as far as his career path choice. I really couldn't figure out just what exactly he did for a living. But in these grainy black and white journals in my possession, these should give me a clue.

I wouldn't be surprised if he now works in a respectful job for the government.. I don't know if he would want his past identity to be known in his present state. I picture Ricky to have a respectful eight to five job. He comes to work in an Aloha shirt tucked into his black dressed pants with black loafers. I have an image of him in his own cubicle and looking at a hypnotizing computer screen.

I hope that someday he would come out and identify himself to solve this mystery. So, from the sordid unauthorized file of Ricky Wang comes this following story.

The reader might be suspicious that there are present day references. But, this is because of the writer's interpretation from the old journals into a kind of new testament version.

REPRESSED MEMORY

Man: Hey Kid, what are you going to be when you grow up?

Kid: Ah, I don't know.

Man Do you know how to get that first good job?

Kid: No

Man: Well, you can do the long route of 4 years at a university, or 2 years in the military, or vocational training, or at an entry level service job here in Hawaii. Then, you have to exaggerate your resume′ on your job interviews. Well kid, I have a short-cut method on landing that first job.

Kid: Is It legal?

Man: Hey, there's a thin line between what's legal and what's not. Even the government will come knocking at your door offering you a position with your surveillance know how. The media will like your paparazzi potential.

Kid: What will I have to do?

Man: Okay, the best jobs aren't in the classifieds. So, you have to manufacture one. Now, here's the plan. Find out who the employers in this town are, and follow them with a hidden camera. Eventually, you'll get something you might be able to blackmail that person with, and the negotiate a deal.

Kid: Are you some kind of guidance counselor?

Man: I'm not a certified licensed instructor, if that's what you mean.

Kid: (In Jail) Bad Advice…Bad Advice (Shaking Head with the "No" Expression)

Narrator: So Remember kids, don't accept advice from strangers.

INTELLIGENCE TEST

Thanks for taking my call. No, I'm not calling a talk radio program. I just made it to the second round. I passed the drug test in the first round. My prize is an interview with the personnel department. The second test is to measure a person's intelligence. But, I'm told that there are no right or wrong answers. I will have to answer with the first thought that comes to my mind of a list of people and things.

Interviewer: "Let's start with Bill Clinton."

Answer: "Whether you like him or not, why can't you pick on somebody your own weight. Okay, that wasn't a good answer. Could this first response be a sample question like in an aptitude test?"

Interviewer: "Hillary Clinton"

Answer: "I don't understand why some people criticize her because she is a feminist. I mean, leave the chick alone."

Interviewer: "Jesus Christ"

Answer: "He's the messiah guy. I wonder what his dad said when he majored in philosophy in college. I think a liberal university made him feel that his socialist view would work in the real world."

Interviewer: "Jimmy Swaggart"

Answer: “He’s the guest host for the vacationing Jesus Christ.”

Interviewer: “Abraham Lincoln”

Answer: “He had a hat-on.”

Interviewer: “Ted Kennedy”

Answer: “He’s the junkest son of the family. If there’s a word such as “junkest.” I can identify with that.”

Interviewer: “Strom Thurmond or Jesse Helms” (Because these two guys are so different)

Answer: “He is super, fantastic, and awesome baby! He is the adult diaper in the political arena, baby!”

Interviewer: “Jane Fonda”

Answer: “If she is a true liberal, why doesn’t she have any adopted Vietcong children? She should have learn the example of adopting disadvantage children set by Mia Farrow.

Interviewer: “Tom Arnold”

Answer: “He’s a plain looking guy, takes Roseanne’s money, and boinks 20 year old women. That kid is American. I like celebrities who made their riches by annoying other people.”

Interviewer: “Roseanne”

Answer: “Why is that woman yelling at me?”

Interviewer: "Margaret Cho"

Answer: "Why is that Asian woman yelling at me?"

Interviewer: "Mike Tyson"

Answer: "I don't know if I will pay to see him fight again, but I would pay to see him in a hetro porn."

Interviewer: "Will Smith"

Answer: "I think he's popular because everybody loves those wise ass generation x-ers."

Interviewer: "O. J. Simpson"

Answer: "I think he misunderstood the 10 Commandments with the three wishes joke where the first two don't count. He might have thought that the first two killings, and not wishes don't count."

Interviewer: "Tesh Rules!"

Answer: "Yeah, a-holes always have power!"

Interviewer: "Vince McMahon"

Answer: " I know that pro wrestling is pushing the limit. But, do they have to use the slogan? Are you ready for some sodomy?"

Interviewer: "Dr. Kevokian"

Answer: "I wouldn't want to be the guy to check if he had cream in his jeans after an assisted suicide."

Interviewer: “Woody Allen”

Answer: “I admired his work, but the step-Oedipus moral character is creepy.”

Interviewer: “Hideo Nomo”

Answer: “If he is released from a Major League Baseball team. His wife will call him Hideo No More Money, No More Honey.”

Interviewer: “Richard Simmons”

Answer: “Did he get arrested for male fraud?”

Interviewer: “Janet Reno”

Answer: “You won’t find male D.N.A in her home.”

Interviewer: “Ally McBeal”

Answer: “Television can make 60 minutes of P.M.S. entertaining.”

Interviewer: “Robert Downey Jr.”

Answer: “I have to see his movies because he needs someone to support his black tar heroin addiction.”

Interviewer: “Sylvester Stallion”

Answer: “He won’t play “Rocky” anymore, instead he will be starring in the Gerry Coney Story.”

Interviewer: “Television Journalism”

Answer: "I will watch Entertainment Tonight only when there's a tragic story or a crime report on a celebrity. It's more interesting than the regular celebrity softball self-promotional questions.

Interviewer: "Who is your favorite actress"

Answer: "She's an actress who critics would define as f—able!"

Interviewer: "Can you name any celebrity who died this past year?"

Answer: "I don't play the dead pool game, because I feel that a famous person who won't tell you if he's dead or not is probably giving you the silent treatment."

Interviewer: "David Letterman"

Answer: "He's the king of irony. It's better than the king of smart ass!"

Interviewer: "Michael Jackson"

Answer: "He's the king of pedophile."

Interviewer: "Bryant Gumble"

Answer: "He's called the whitest black-man. Who's the blackest white-man?

Interviewer: "Rush Limbaugh"

Answer: "He speaks for a generation. From a loan shark from God, here he comes!"

Interview: “Alan Greenspan”

Answer: “He’s a mind gym teacher.”

Interviewer: “This concludes your interview, and you don’t have to stick around for the results. I think you know how well you did.”

SKILLS

Work Ethic

Ricky worked so hard that there's white stuff coming out around his mouth after a day's work.

Gaps In Employment

Why are their breaks in your continuity of employment? The male likely possibility is of being a drug dealer. The female possibility is of being a prostitute.

Ricky's Good Points

What are my hobbies? I like sports, music, reading, and I also like to bark at the moon. Is that a problem?

If you don't like what I'm saying so far, you can talk to the hand job.

I'm not bragging, but I can kiss ass 24-7.

I shouldn't state this in the interview, but I'm battling my demons!

I can say "hey baby" in a high voice.

I knew that before I was born. I'll say that to every question asked of me.

I can suck my teeth during lunch breaks.

I can grit my teeth till it becomes annoying.

I can smack my mouth while eating.

I can break pencils in between my fingers.

I have the ability to be bored and have a dialog at the same time.

I have the ability to psychological damage the people who work with me.

I have the skill to be a bench-warmer.

I'm really humble, that's why I keep my talent to myself.

Job Opportunities

Having washboard abs. You can do gay porn!

Athletic skill- Unfortunately, it is of a bowler or billiards player. I like to perform on the job where you can have a cigarette or a beer during the work time.

Negotiator- I can trace my ancestors to the agent for Adam who negotiated with God to make sex feel good.

Job Listings

Sportscaster- I blew it by saying that one player was waived or cut more times than an O. J. Simpson's ex-wife.

Psychiatrist- My advice to everything is "yeah, so." My prognosis to everyone's opinion is, "You're sick!"

A Revolutionary- But, it didn't even pay minimum wage.

Salesperson- I didn't want to sell anything. I changed my mind on a sales by saying, "no, it's mine," and kept it.

Newscaster- I prepared myself too much by excessively saying "thank you."

Announcer- I can read the Penthouse letters to illiterates.

Commissioner- If I can't be a commissioner of anything, I'll just pout and be an anarchist.

Entertainer- I can wear a chicken suit. I want to say, "pluck me!"

Investigative reporter- I can't do controversial issues, so I will have to investigate the obvious wrongs.

Cowboy- I would like to be a cowboy, except that I believe that horses have rights too.

Casting Director- Where am I going to find a casting directing school for the necessary training for that type of position? Which has higher standards, Hamburger College or a Casting Directing license?

There would be no casting couch if the person in charge of casting would have to pay up front to applicants.

Local Television Program Director- This job might be considered kind of a nepotism job. But you have to be innovated to come up with original ideas such as hiring a beauty contestant to do the weather, or hiring your girlfriend to read the sports off the teleprompter.

Public Worker's Union Leader- I can be a head of a union. All I need is a manual that I can follow. It states that your union threatens to strike in an election year for a better contract which the previous contract just happens to end at every election year.

An Athlete's Agent- You suggested to a player like Keyshawn Johnson to improve his marketability. He should trash talk about an undersize, overachieving, blue-collar white guy in a professional sport.

Not In the Listings

Your career is to have a baby with a pro athlete. She can make a six figure income for the first eighteen years of the child's life.

Business Environment

Ricky will look for a business with a lot of fat guys employees. This signals an easy job. But, those jobs are hard to get.

Those high paying male dominated fields are also hard to get. When they go on strike. They will say that the pay raise is deserved in relation to the rising cost of living. They can't say that the pay increase during
the negotiations is for "going to see strippers" money.

Touch By An Angel

Isn't that spiritual harassment in the workplace?

Ricky's Working Conditions

What do you mean? When I can't say, "as long as I don't have to bend over," to the boss.

Am I annoying the other workers, if I want them to "guess" on whatever I asked something.

I can identify with newscasters and other careers people would kill for, who complain about working on holidays.

It's a good career when there's a box score on your day's work.

Non-verbal Skill

Ricky claims that he can change human form. So, if there's a hide and seek competition job. I'm there, or not.

Surveillance

Ricky is a little into the spying on others with the neighborhood watch thing. He has a crystal ball. Oops, it's the wrong time to be looking into that person's life while he's doing that.

He can figure out who farted, but that isn't being considered as having detective ability at the time.

The Untouchables

Ricky wanted to be in an union because he hated a pop quiz that can get him a failing grade. That's the purpose of paying dues, so that he won't have to take tests and not be fired no matter what. Even a politician wouldn't like to be ambushed with geography questions.

Resume′

When you send a picture with your application. That's a sexual harassment suit waiting to happen.

Job Performance-Don'ts

Don't ANALyze me.

First Amendment-Ricky's Freedom of Speech

have the right to say anything until I get fired.

never do that, because I don't know how.

disagree with everyone, because nobody tells what to do.

will control myself to just say "no" instead of "s— no."

can say, "okay, what else!" to any suggestions.

answer sarcastically, "yeah, I can read" to anything asked of me.

can shrug my shoulders when I pretend not to know something. This is my selective ignorance is bliss.

will describe every colleague in the workplace as a self-promoting person.

can't say, "you're not the boss hog of me" to authority anymore.

want to know beforehand about the escape routes at the job site.

won't say "beg me" when my boss wants my to do something.

will end every conversation to a fellow worker with "you understand" to what I just said.

want to work with someone who is constantly smirking.

After a compliment, I'll say, "tell me something I don't know."

You can't tell me anything without the response of "make me."

I'm known as the "wasn't me" guy.

I'm good at stating a sarcastic thank you. I want to be in a business where you can sarcastically say, "Can I help you?"

It is not a good idea to forget your resume′ on an interview. Then, when asked to verbalized your job experience. You say that you could tell him, but you will have to kill him.

Paranoid

Ricky is known as the "side-eye" guy at the workplace.

He thinks that everything that happens in the office is a set-up of some kind.

Not the Right Time

To make myself at home, I will use self-deprecating humor during a private meeting with a critical boss.

Casting Call

That's the only place where you can ask an applicant to turn around and let me have a better look at you.

Legality

Ricky can't tell the difference between discrimination and screening people.

Parental Skills

Ricky learned to end each statement with, "moron, dummy, or fool."

Drug Testing

They shouldn't have drug testing in the workplace. Public schools wouldn't have shop teachers if alcoholism is considered substance abuse.

Major Wood-shop

You wanted to be a substitute teacher for wise-ass students where Richard Hurts rules.

Optional

You applied to become a naked waiter. Will you check if the coffee is hot enough?

Psychic Hot-line

An advantage of having a long last name is that I know immediately that it is a sales call from a telemarketer slowly trying to pronounce my last name wrongly. I could say that person doesn't live here anymore, and when asked what's my name. I will state an ethnic name who's stereotyped for not paying their bills.

There should be a fee attached to an unsolicited phone call. I'm an unlicensed attorney, so my time will cost you.

Go Into Another Field

You can't be a Gynecologist when your first name is Nick. It won't be comfortable for a woman if his nickname is "Nick the Clit."

The Computer Guy

Ricky was being kind of an a-hole at the job site because he thought he was an essential employee.

Whenever he saw a male co-worker talking to a female co-worker. Ricky would repeat what he said in a "Beavis &Butthead voice, and yell that's sexual harassment.

Coyote Colleague

You're in a field where you don't remember having an attractive co-worker.

Freedom Fighters

You can update your resume′ in the free world.

Pension

Will they retire my number along with my name tag?

Perfect

You have the face for writing television show

MEDIOCRE NIHLISM

There was a question Ricky thought about when he was a kid. Can I be a rebel, and not be attractive in some sense at the same time? Because as a kid, looks are the most important part in a superficial world. He thought that being an anarchist would be rebellious. But he was a latch-key kid, so it resulted in breaking his own stuff. Ricky was the leader of his own club, but with no membership. He made a flyer with the slogan "Let's Party!" The only feedback that he received was from a Marxist guy who wouldn't shaddup and leave his place. He tried to play by his own rules, but he felt that it's too self promoting. He had no idea what constitutes being a rebel. So, Ricky has some opinions to what makes a rebel under some different headings.

Clothes Makes the Rebel

I used to wear hand me down T-shirts with holes in them and dried up snot from the previous wearers. This relic by the armpit was a vintage classic from the circa year (____).

Hair Makes the Man

I have long sideburns that goes with my tattoos.

Wheels

I had a junk-a-lug car. It had dents to give it character. That piece of crap was cool in public high school. Because it showed toughness for some reason. The coolness lasted in college for the first two years. Then the real world outside of school spoiled it, when appearance mattered in a materialistic environment.

___Job

I thought that being a rebel is having a low paying job.

Commercialize Rebellion

That's rock n roll.

Ladder Up

That kiss ass guy moved on up, because he rebelled against the rebellious and not the boss.

Timing is Everything

The rebellious things you used to do. You're considered psychotic when you display that kind of behavior at an older age.

Save Face

"I didn't leave, I got kicked out." That sounds cool when you were in bubble-gum rock band. Your parents set a curfew. But your friends left you too early, and you walked around and waste time till past the deadline. I joined a team, so I can rebel against a coach.

Sexist Rebel

This comes from a male perspective, I would say that it's not shaving her armpits, legs, and upper lip.

Reason

I can use the excuse of being anti-establishment. But, I can't say that I can't do anything right.

Conformity

If you're rebels. Why are you guys dressed in the same uniforms?

Accomplishment

You were a loner in high school. But how did you get away with your classmates not knowing you.

Sold Out

Your rebellious years are supposed to end when your serious love interest arrives on the scene.

DOMESTIC VIOLENCE & CHILD ABUSE AWARENESS

I never saw my father hit or raised his voice at my mother. If he did, it must have been behind closed doors, and they must have been really good at hiding it from us. My dad hit me only one time. Looking back, it was my fault. When he came into my bedroom one day, and saw the mess that I made. He told me to clean up the room. But, I was at the age where you mock people by repeating everything that person says in a silly voice. After I did this brilliant act, he struck me across the mouth with an open hand. As blood dripped at the side of my mouth, I wanted to cry out loud. But the usually fake cry won't work when it's your fault. The look of horror on my dad's face after he saw what he had done. But he couldn't say he was sorry because he was in the right.

So, he just left the room without saying anything. My silent scream signaled a time to grow up in the world. Children learn by examples. When your father respects your mother. Their children will respect their parents and other people.

Ricky can't relate to the kid's today with their mom's boyfriend living with them.

Belief Choice

Am I spiritual? If I had a choice. I would pick a slacker religion. I don't have to be ambitious because the world is going to end soon, anyway.

The Monkee's Theme

There is a line in the Hey, Hey, We're the Monkee's theme, which states "We're too busy singing to put anybody down." Okay, what's the point. Isn't the point of life, we like to judge other people?

Hell's Bells

Is the term "Great Satan" an insult? The "Great Satan" sounds evil, but it also has a cool identity. You want to scare a boy to do good. You can threaten him with a wussy compliment in front of his friends.

Sound Advice

When an expert claims that she is, "I'm my son's mother." That is false modesty bull if I ever heard one.

The New, New Testament

In the revised edition of the Bible, Jesus will address his disciples with more usage of the phrase, "you know what I'm saying," in his speeches.

Alien Culture

Teenagers who are not embarrassed by their parents.

Throw Back Uniform

Parents who suggest a thing called "walking" to a child.

Moral Cleansing

You watched too much porn. Your punishment is to wash your eyes with soap.

Story of Being Poor

He couldn't afford real earrings, so he had to use clothespins on his ears.

Blessing in Disguise

Ricky had a bedwetting problem, it kept him from joining the cub or boy scouts. But, he was lucky. He was kind of a cute kid. Michael Jackson could have been his scoutmaster.

Hurt Feelings

"I don't like him. He called me names." That's basically what goes on in a self-esteem world.

Style Section

You want the shocking look that will stop your entranced into Disneyland.

You Didn't Do It?

Ricky remained a virgin throughout high school. "Damn You High School, Damn You to Hell!"

Dated Movie Classic

Ricky was in his puberty when he saw "The Graduate." He had a boner all night after seeing a topless Mrs. Robinson. It would be difficult for a young boy to achieve the same reaction with all the porn out there.

Evolution of a Male

As a kid, you settle differences on the playground. As a young man, you don't show up because you have better things to do. As an adult, the winner gets arrested for assault.

What's Wrong With the Kid's Today

They are not scared of the religious elderly lady who lives down the street. Now-days, the kids will smirk at anything she says, instead of just politely nodding in agreement.

RICKY'S Y2K plus (YOUTH 2 KID)

Only the Good Die Young

Western culture has always celebrated youth. That explains why Jesus who died in his early thirties is more popular than Moses, who died in his hundreds.

The Good Son

It's a benefit for some people to have a person like Jeffrey Dahmer. You can tell your parents and say, "I'm not a bad son now."

First Love

Name withheld had his first crush on a school teacher. He saw her later, and she kind of put on a few pounds. He couldn't believe that he spanked his monkey to her image. He met her a few years ago in person, and that thing still went boooiiinnnggg.

Surprised

My parents were the shy and quiet types. I thought I could get away with doing embarrassing stuff. But, they will talk to each other. "Oh no, busted!" Next stop, being grounded.

Youth Culture

A trend in show business is to have 20 year old writers. It takes talent to write a sappy dialogue and have rock songs in the background for the UPN Network. I would like to see a young person try to write an episode of Law & Order.

Commercial

From the producers of television is good comes, "Lung cancer from smoking is cool!"

Respect

You try to say to your father, "I'll listen to you when you stop bitchin'!" So, after you picked yourself off the ground. What did he say?

Caged Community

This is not a youth town if it's considered a rich community. In most cases, older people have money.

Fantasy

I don't know how realistic those teen sex movies are, but I was too lazy for those kinds of shenanigans.

Skin to Tie

The manner in how you're dressed, you'll will be stared at by male adolescents.

Paradox

I know it wasn't talked about in the past. But, I don't think masturbating is being ahead of your time.

Clean-cut

I didn't understand how the cheerleaders at the other schools would do gyrations and doing the grind during their cheers. I wanted to transfer there, except I didn't have talent to be recruited by them.

Those Dam Kids, Get Out of My Yard and Street

Oh no, it's those darn punks on mopeds again!

Parallel Universe

Those students who sat at the back of the class correlate to being the first in line at the cafeteria lunch line.

Reward

I don't get dessert because of what I did! You mean there's not enough room for Jell-O after a joke.

Name in the Paper

Where were you at the time of that incident mentioned in the newspaper crime report?

Big Boy

You're not hurt, you just have to put some rubbing alcohol on it. You have learn to play with pain.

Lesson in Confined Self-discovery

You're not in jail. You're just stubborn, and locked yourself in your room.

Taunting

"Na, Na, I saw an older person scold you!"

Fables

Things were better in the old days, because you were better looking during those times.

Early Popularity Contest

I stuffed the Christmas card ballot box by writing to myself under different assume names, and also dead kids were included for the inflated numbers.

No Excuses

You beat me, because you're heavier and smellier.

Hold It In

I can't drink beer before school starts, because I don't want to use the high school bathrooms.

Macho Man

Guys don't say, "Oh, that's cute!"

Grow-up

I'm getting too old for detention. I have to move on up to bigger and better things.

Cable Television Comes to Town

I was shocked to see Mork swearing, "Nanu, Nanu, you F-ing, s—!"

Send Money

I was sent fake money, or what is now called credit cards. A conspiracy theorist would call it the Federal Reserve's phony currency.

Life Is a Picnic

A kid is happy to eat outside. He thinks that it's roughing it for a nuclear family. But to a homeless family, it's called eating time.

Future Planner

A slacker high school student will schedule his class to be in the classroom closest to the cafeteria before the lunch-time break, and will schedule his 6th period class to be in the classroom closest to the parking lot.

You Think You're Better Than Me

I resented the kid who could converse with adults. Does that kid think we aren't as smart as he think he is?

Nothing to Lose-Rather Be Where

I hated the troublemaker who lived close to school, so he didn't mind when we had to stay after school.

Mundane Life

You think life is boring when you're young. You will have a lot more time later to have a tired life.

Social Promotion

Your 5 years as a senior in high school are, the first was being drunk, the second was being on drugs, the third is spent sleeping, the fourth was in rehab watching television, and the fifth was done in a last minute manner.

Strict Mom

She put ex-lax in your dinner, so you wouldn't go out at night.

Pro Choice

You're torn between having a rich or poor girlfriend, because of what kind of eats there are at her home.

Report Card

What kind of kid was I? I was the worst kind of youngster. "I know it, you know it, the family knows it!"

You Can't Go Home Again

The high school beauty could have done a lot more with that face. When I went back there, I saw a child with similar features of hers, and that reminds me that I'm getting older.

Barber Chop

He is called a barber and not a hair-stylist, because he had that smile after cutting your hair too short.

Teachers

Kids don't have imagination. I was scolded by teachers when I daydreamed in school. I thought that daydreaming was using my creative skills.

Annoyed

The bully liked to annoy the shy kid with, “come on, let’s talk about sex!”

Manhood

After being scared, a teenager will start swearing excessively and say, “yeah, I’m still tough!”

The Other Half

The girls in the smart class will dress conservatively, and the girls in the lower phase classes will dressed scantily. You almost wanted to have lower tests scores, in order to be in those 2 drink minimum classes.

Crime &Punishment

Your punishment for any wrong doing is to pull weeds around the campus. But, it’s an urban school without greenery anywhere.

Nickname

Your nickname in high school is what your father does for a living.

Universal Story

It seems like every parent has a when I was you age, I was poor. There had to be rich parents somewhere!

A Boy’s Thing

We can call each other by our last names. Girls don't have the same affects of toughness by doing that.

Where's the Party?

The ideal party for parents is for their kids to bring their homework with them.

Keep It to Yourself

When her brother is prettier. Are you gay? I'm going to tell everybody what you said.

Church Rules

I can't stop giggling when the minister states that, "Not to covet your neighbor's ass."

Play Acting

In front of your home, your father will terrorize you to scare the neighbors not to go into the yard.

Embarrass

I will need to have mom's permission before I can do something dangerous.

Grownup

I will be doing things later in life, which I despised as a youth.

Mountain Man

I didn't clean up my room, because I wanted to conserve water and save the environment.

Birth Control

My parents regretted the big age difference between the kids. Because later in life, the younger kid will look like he could be the older one's kid.

Duct Tape

I don't see that anymore. The parents will put tape across the mouth of the kid who makes too much noise. Unless, a child's hands are tied behind his back. The tape is easy to take off, but the fear of taking it off is greater than the punishment.

Status

Your name appears in the newspaper after you've been arrested for drunk driving.

Convinced Into Early Gambling Addiction

I can get another classmate to do anything just by saying, "I bet you won't do it."

Kids in America

You can enjoy your free time by doing or not doing wasting time stuff.

Diet

As a kid, my diet consists of eating junk food. Hopefully, I'll become so tired of it. I'll will be eating those ethnic acquired food meals as an adult.

Lesson Learned

After you show your tongue, which is regarded as bad manners. Your mother will try to stop you from doing that again by putting red peppers on your tongue. It will keep burning and burning.

Union

Kids will strike by not doing homework. This is a form of career preparation for being in the real world of the workplace where being on strike is a necessity.

Class Struggle

I made the other kids guilty by saying that your parents make more money than mine. Then, I will spout off some kind of an attempt at pre-college Marxism.

Pop Quiz

A teacher doesn't want to be graded. Union dues and a teaching certificate are preventive measures for not wanting to take another exam.

Qualifications

Do you have a well-read instructor if he doesn't catch a student plagiarizing his term papers. I thought that's what encyclopedias are created for copying.

Too Deep For Public School

I didn't pass love notes in high school, but I passed out notices for some revolutionary meetings at the neighborhood center.

We're Talkin' Proud

You bragged that your high school had more welfare families than any other in the state.

Role Model

Your idol can't be younger than you.

Silence Is Golden

Sleeping won't get you into trouble. But sleeping with someone is another story.

Bad Timing

The worse time to get sick is during the holidays or on summer vacation.

Owe Them

You should remember to be good to your parents who wiped your ass as a baby.

Shame (Make "A" Stuff)

I can't talk about girlfriend stuff to my parents.

Chase Scene

The bully will run after you to rub some kind of stink stuff on you.

Old School Porn

As a kid, I went to the barber shop because of the calendar featuring topless women.

Difference a Brain Makes

I couldn't figure out what's the difference of being lovesick and what's a social disease.

Depression

To a kid, depression is the anticipation on a Sunday night or towards the end of the weekend before school starts again for the week. You also have the same down feeling during the Jerry Lewis telethon, which signals the end of summer vacation and the start of a new school year.

Naïve

I lost of my innocence when I'm not embarrassed anymore after I see a pregnant classmate.

Gym Class

I can't respect the king or queen of the high school prom after seeing either one of them in the shower.

Cool

We have obscene nicknames for each other.

Just Say Yes

Drugs are good when they are used by your classmates, which resulted in a lower class curve.

Attendance

The thing you missed most about high school are those cheap government subsidized school lunches.

Be Patient

You're told that you have to wait till you're a grownup before you can have any form of power. But, you're used to instant products. A short attention span person wants it now.

Political Correctness

Parents can't say, "are you deaf?" when scolding their kid. Even if the child pretends not to hear them. This question as a statement is an insult to hearing impaired people.

Useful Against a Person Who Won't Leave

Your dad doesn't want that guy coming into his home again, so he wants you to play with him aggressively. He's an adult, so he can't hit a kid back, or there will be a lawsuit.

Grand Master Debater

I can't out talk the smart kid without threatening to smack him.

Too Much Times This Month

My excuse for not attending school the previous day is of a personal relationship nature, which I don't need doctor's note.

Show Business Parents

Superficial parents who ask you, "who do you want to look like when you grow up?"

Smart Ass

A student who tells the history teacher that he doesn't buy what was just stated in his lecture, even when the material is from the so-called non-fiction history books.

Lack of Maturity

Boys who challenge each other on whose clothes are more soiled.

Say What!

Your boyhood idol was Rocky Balboa, and not Rocky Balwhore.

Kid's Show

An adult star of a children's show tries to be cute by asking a boy if he has a girlfriend. In an era of political correctness, he has to change girlfriend to partner.

Blame

I thought I was born for the purpose of my dad having someone to yell at, when he couldn't fix something.

Roy Tokashiki

Eye In the Sky

I regretted being raised in a small town because it didn't prepare me to drive in a traffic of a city.

Retard

My nickname was the name of the local mental hospital.

Cult Jam

The mantra this early cult used was of Gary Numan's one hit where, "The only way to live is in Cars."

Puberty

Name withheld had his first heart on to Racquel Welch in any movie that she appeared in color.

Own Place

I don't have to worry when something around the house is accidentally damaged. Of course, it's the early first place's cheap kind of stuff.

Reverse Universe

It was cooler to be older in high school. In the adult world, it is cooler to be younger.

Mean Streets

That pre-teen series on a weekend afternoon has street talk with straight A-students.

Height Matters

I hit myself on the head. The purpose of this is to create lumps in order to be taller.

Betting Line

I will ask a history teacher to not tell the results of a battle. "It's close your eyes time," I want to know the odds on the Ottoman line.

Music Do the Talkin'

The music in a church is much cheaper than an expensive rock band concert.

Short Memory

I can't remember the names of the teachers in high school or college anymore. Am I getting old, or I don't remember the names of people who can't help me anymore? I'm too self-centered to waste space in my little used brains.

A.M or F.M

I missed my prom because I thought that event was a day game.

Doomsday

I accidentally damaged something in a Sunday school class.

Ring of Fire

The only attention I received as a kid was of being laughed at by bullies.

Badge of Honor

I was kicked out of the Junior Police Officer because I roughed up a jaywalker.

Didn't Mind

You can call me a fag as long as I can go out with your well-built sister.

Conservative Family-No Nipple Rule

The sons of that family kept their tops on at all times. No nipples of any gender will be shown in public.

Popular

A child star will have to smoke a lot of cigarettes or masturbate frequently in order to stunt his growth. He doesn't want to hear that he isn't cute anymore by being too tall on the television screen.

Heaven

I remembered when my parents changed from a black and white to a color television. I had the opportunity to see hot actresses in their flesh color skin.

Warning

A classmate will sit next to you and say, "I don't bite." It's better than me because "I suck!"

Favoritism

Which one of the two children will their parents favor? The one who is a punk, or the other one who is a hippie.

No Books

What kind of class doesn't have homework? Let me take a guess. There are probably pregnant girls in that class.

Boss

Your mom teaches you proper etiquette. But, she tells you to "move" instead of saying excuse me." It's cute when she states an order in an accent.

Small Town

I didn't have sex in high school. I knew these girls as classmates from small kid time. It's "eeaahh" coming from both sides.

Protective

I'm embarrassed when my parents are in the same room during a shock jock saying offensive things.

Black Market Name Brand

How much did you spend to get that rebellious look?

Proud Day

I'm surprised that the bad guys in high school knew your name.

Student Manager

No one listens to you. The only task you have is to chase foul balls.

Self-Praising

You can't call your daughter princess. You made yourself a king, which is unintentionally funny in today's cynical world.

Revenge

You should never pick on a nerdy kid who's good at science.

Let Down

You had an encounter with your hero, and he's an obnoxious spoiled bastard.

King

The reason you became a father is that you're never wrong to someone now.

Just Right

I have to watch out for the guy who's the same size as me. He can steal my clothes.

You Want It?

No impostor will even want take your job or change places with you.

Peaked

Who brags about being popular in high school? It's like bragging about being born with an imitation silver spoon in your mouth.

Good Excuse

I can't do my homework, if there's a threat of a looming nuclear holocaust on the horizon.

Wrong Message

I think the message in "Pinocilio" of your nose growing larger with every lie is the wrong idea to send. Instead, each lie would result in having a thing becoming smaller. This would be a more effective message for a young man.

Con

I've been a victim of a rock n roll swindle. I bought this CD at a local franchise for a couple more dollars than at Tower's.

Boy's Fight

I will never say, "I'll scratch your eyes out!"

PETA Out

I kept these little plastic bags to suffocate cockroaches, and a magnifying glass to burn ants. These activists will throw blood at fur wearing old ladies, but won't throw blood on fur wearing pimps.

Manhood

I won't carpool with girls in case the car breaks down. They will expect me to fix the problem because I'm the male, so I'm supposed to know what the problem is.

Lesson

I can't use that, "didn't your parents teach you right from wrong?" speech to him. They were too naïve. The concept of being an a-hole was my own idea. No one can teach me that kind of rude behavior.

False Accusation

The loudmouth who calls you a racist is like the trouble-making kid. He made up stuff that you said in order to get you into fights.

Haircut

I used the "Jesus" excuse, when my parents wanted me to cut my hair. If Jesus could have long hair. Why can't I?

Preparation Dance

"Put your hands in the air!" is a dance movement or what you say during an armed robbery.

Smell Regression

That bad smell bring back bad memories.

Slacker Religion

I didn't mind going to Sunday school because there are no exams or homework that will be graded.

Motivational Listener

I wanted to become a high school teacher, just to hear the music from a high school band.

Category

It's stretching the educational standards, when sitcoms are considered documentaries in a child's viewer's curriculum.

Poet

My poems are mostly about butterflies, and the book of poems includes an ironed dead butterfly in it.

Ahead of Its Time

I was called, "Elephant man" before the movie came out in theaters.

Name Change

The Home Economics class changed its title to be more gender friendly for the boys by calling the class as "single guy living."

Practical Joke

I used my friend's name to request a sappy song on a local radio station.

Sound Effects

I bought beer in glass bottles instead of aluminum ones, because I want to hear the glass breaking sound when it's thrown onto the roads.

Not Healthy

Puberty is a time when you can actually pop stuff growing on your face. Later in life, you should have it checked by a doctor.

Life Is Good

As a kid in a tourist economy, you see tourists walking around and tell your parents that you want to become a tourist when you grow older. But, a tourist isn't considered as a career.

Non-Sweet

Your kid hasn't drink that kind of liquid in his life? You must be referring to "water."

Public Relations

That rock n roll radio station had their remote location at a teen gang-banger location.

Natural High

Press your eyes real hard to see kaleidoscope stars! This is before video games and is much cheaper.

Example

Your alcohol impaired high school counselor tells you that, "you will always be a loser!"

Retro

The public school cafeteria food idea is about as brilliant as the Planet Hollywood concept. Will the menu comprised of subsidized food at a higher cost? The local teen hang-out is located by a banded chemical manufacturing plant. The local teen gang consists of kids with receding hairlines.

Early Stardom

I appeared on the local kid's program, "Kids who are losers." They wouldn't accept any kids with criminal records, because that will be considered cheating for that show.

Comeback Kid

I was on the debating team. But during a losing argument, I would call the opponent, "Mr. Know it all."

Pre-Maturity

His parents won't have to tell him to wash his own bed sheets.

The 1980's

The Hello Kitty stores are the same thing as "selling pussy." Okay, who put this in the book.

Nutrition

Fast foods are good for you because the U.S.A has the best athletes.

Stunts

Kids, “don’t try this at home!” I cut off a part of my own body, so it can replaced with a bionic one.

Same Answer

Your parents are there to say that you “waste money” to everything that you want to buy.

Grow Out of It

There’s a problem, if you talk like a kid when speaking with the blowing air out of his nose and making soft bubbles sound.

18 and Life

How do women celebrate turning 18? They wouldn’t do the same stuff as a male by heavy drinking after the birthday party. She will puke out her birthday cake. That’s a bulimia’s dream.

Weapons

Kids have a too easy access to guns. So during a confrontation, instead of using guns, can’t you two just spit at each other.

Male Son

I didn’t ask my parents how they first met. I’m a boy.

Curfew

Your mother has different kinds of yelling, if you’re late from school, and if you’re late from a date.

Commercialism

In the high school yearbook, classmates should have the opportunity to plug products in their photo.

Shyness

He is so afraid of girls as a young man that he will hide in the chicken coop. Being with other chickens would be appropriate for him.

Stressed

There's more pressure from your parents when they say to "have fun."

Too Protected

Your parents advice to everything is, "you're not ready for anything!"

Manners

I might be able to get away with saying "yeah," but not f—, yeah!"

Superficial Thing

Who do you want to look like when you grow up?

B.C (Before Childhood)

I hate to think how you behaved before you've supposed to have matured.

Parental Guidance

Whose kid is that? What kind of "fool parents" would let that kid do that?

Father's Day

You wanted to thank your dad for not foolin' around like those fathers on television.

Seriously

I was unintentionally funny at school. It is funnier because I wasn't trying to be funny.

Arrange Clothes

This section in the closet is for the egg stained shirts.

We Don't Need Another Zero

My super-hero is really watered down now compared to those spider-man days.

At the Shopping Mall

She'll will be listening to some teen heart-trob and drinking diet soda.

Blue Collar Dad

You made how much for that job? You can't buy s— with that much!

Pocket Expense

Your parents gave you some jail money allowance.

Brains on Drugs

I was surprised that the high school stoned guy remembered my name!

Slow Motion

I have to break the previous record time, when my dad calls me on his first yell.

Chariots of the Gods

I can't step on insects. They might be our ancient astronauts.

Goals

I'll try to maintain the same haircut for all of my life. Basically, a person strives to get more of the share.

Cheap Surgery

When the bully threatens me with a fat lip, I won't need the collagen injections.

Wear This

You're not living with your parents. So, you can't say your mother made you wear that.

Same Designer

You brought your old clothes with you to your own place.

Shiny Special People

In high school, kids left alone the special guy who walked around carrying a porn magazine out in the open. He wasn't picked on because he's psychotic or special.

Lived Through a World War

Your grandparents could wear the same old clothes. But, children aren't allowed to do that because their favorite old clothes were tossed in the garbage.

Public School Number

That's a cheap high school, when they won't allowed tackle football because they don't have insurance. You had a socialist high school football coach who felt that there is no fighting in football.

P.S.A. No Shame

Endorsements are made by successful people who didn't have sex in high school.

Time-line

You're getting older when the actresses you followed in your youth are slowly having their voices becoming lower every time you see them.

Isolated Small Town

There is nothing to do. So, you'll eat before going to sleep in hope of having nightmares, because that's the only excitement that you'll have.

Innocence Lost

I lost my innocence about the time that I stop using crayons.

Useless Protector

My super-hero can only stop a bullet when it's not fired from a gun.

Skunk Alarm

His parents went away for the weekend. That left their teenage son alone at home. So, to prevent him from throwing a party. They sprayed something in the house that would stink throughout the weekend.

No Need for Book Learning

I don't need textbooks. I get all my facts from a friend and from hearsay.

Cliché

How old are you? I hear that after I made some sort of mistake.

Wait till Next Year

I left my Christmas presents unopened so that the wrapping has a brown tint to them. I'm just not excited, because I know what they are without unwrapping them.

Missing Wife and Pop Store

I'm afraid of going into that store, because he is a madman who wants to rule the world in his mind.

Braggart

My parents swear more than yours.

Watch Your Language

Could you not call everything as "s—?"

Really Pathetic

When you're not good enough to get beat up by bullies.

1984, Merry Christmas

Santa Claus will be watching you.

That's Not Cute

My pet is so scared when I stroke it that it will urinate at the same time in a sweeping motion of a hose.

Not a Pretty Mess

Hurry up! You have a time limit for urinating during commercials.

Good Advice

The key to success is to do some thinking, and not some f-ing.

Recent Member

When you started to date his daughter, it was about the same time that he joined the N.R.A..

I Know the Look

That kid is making that "stubborn boy face."

Indoor Football

You're just out of the shower, and use the roll-up towel as a football. You play the quarterback and run the option, and your friend grabbed the wrong ball.

The 70's Look

I will constantly rub my eyes to get the red eyes look.

Shakespeare High

What is he saying? He must be on hallucinations.

End of an Era

You supposed to avert your eyes in a bowing manner when you meet a rich person. Now, you give a mean stare.

Kids Know

They don't want to go with you to a meeting or a bank. You can't buy goodies at these places.

In-complain, 2nd down

You're sick and tired. Don't you have to see a doctor or get some rest?

Tardy Slip

The excuse you used for tardiness is to be fashionable late.

D.P Standards

Do what I say, and not as I did.

PG-pre 60's

In those old movies, there are no blood but a lot of internal bleeding. They must have been tougher then.

Servants Without Freedom

You're a little too old to be a slave to a high school senior.

Cruel and Unusual Punishment

I have to lick the fly-swatter as my punishment.

Greasy Kid Stuff

A cutting kid has that "McDonalds and you're not in class" odor during school hours.

Blair Witch Project Phenomenon

The younger generation where most of them want to be a star. Tom Green is an amateur God in TV land.

Video-cam

Contrived plots are considered real in a M.T.V generation.

Wash Me

You fog the car windows with your breath, and then write stuff with your fingers.

Previous Generation

You don't get or understand the popularity of a new celebrity. You realize your own comb over style.

Your Stein Back to the Wall

You had a retarded friend in high school because he had unknown strength and was a good fighter against anyone who tried to bully you. A strong mentally challenge kid with a good heart is a deterrent against school bullies. A bully is scared of fighting a mentally challenged boy who fights in an unorthodox manner and never gives up. He wouldn't hold back in hitting a bully who's younger and smaller, and have no hesitation against a girl bully who thought he wouldn't fight her because she's a girl.

High in High School

He will say mean things about drug addicts because they bullied him in high school.

After School Special

Teenagers need immigrants. Mom and Pop store owners are the only places where an underage person can buy cigarettes without pretending not to understand your fake I.D.

Aroma-therapy

I remembered that place as smelling like sun-baked urine.

Smart-Ass Rules

The "Be a Man" cliché doesn't work on a male who really just wants to be a guy.

No Nick at Nite for You

I can't watch Happy Days. I now realize that Fonzie was a creepy older guy who hung around high school students. You see a person like that in real life. You call the local authorities if there has been any sex offenders moving into the neighborhood. (See The Mark Chrmura in Milwaukee Story)

High Ticket Prices

A lesson learned for a teenager to afford to see high priced entertainers is to be a drug dealer. Who else could make that much to be able to afford a ticket?

No TV at Home, Go Door to Door

He's the neighborhood religious kid who the only movie he saw was The Ten Commandments. (I'm supposed to become more cynical as I get older. But I'm in tears when watching those Bible stories, which didn't happen when I was a kid watching those movies.)

Sticky Merit Badges

Ricky's friend wanted to join the Boy Scouts because he wanted to pitch a tent.

Skewed Belief

Your elders told you not to steal from others, because their dead ancestors will haunt you and give you bad luck. But, if you're stealing from someone. Chances are that person is a loser, and the odds are that all his failures will be attributed to his bad luck, according to him.

Electronic Discipline

"Go to Your Room" isn't punishment. Parents should send their misbehave kid to his room after turning the "off" switch to his room in the circuit breaker.

End of Debate

You can't convince your father in a conversation about the contradictions in life. His reply is, "Yeah, that's a double standard. Deal with it!"

Movie Fights

It's two against one, but you can take on those two pretty boys. You have nothing to loose.

Wise Words

Ricky's father told him that a person shouldn't talk too much. When you speak, make it important. Ricky's dad may have said that or not, he didn't say much.

Voting With Your Pocketbook

You're a grown-up and left the nest when you bought something over $1000 with your own money.

WHISKEY TALKIN'

Ricky's personal file

Hyphenated Word

I thought fake is a pre-fix to the word "orgasm."

Virgin Territory

I have in my hand something that is non-scented, and smells fresh like unused genitalia. She has the new girl smell.

Tour Guide

While walking down a Waikiki street, you see a tourist from the Far East and ask. "Is that Shishido on your face, or are you glad to see me?"

Fiancee

Why doesn't she think my mother will like her? Is it because of the being an alleged slut rumor that she is worried my mother might have heard?

Ego

My girlfriend left me. Am I angry because I care about her, or that she thinks the other guy is a better man than me?

Mr. Right

You can't meet a good man. Is it because the men you see, just want to have sex? Wait, that's me.

Equality

The single woman in her 40's will have a change in her appeal. Her physical appearance isn't important as her financial status. In other words, she becomes a man.

One Thing Leads to Another

You're a nihilist because you're not getting laid.

On the Surface

Your breakup is much more serious than mine. The last relationship I was involved in my mind. She just greeted me with, "hi honey." That doesn't sound too deep and too one-sided.

For Your Protection

Television isn't bad for you. It can be used with instructions and a VCR to provide safe sex.

Storybook

When I meet a potential girlfriend. I will ask her if we could start praying together, even if it's in a place like a bar. In case, we should marry and have children. We could tell our kids that we meet while we were praying.

Sensual

You don't see a stripper doing the robot dance. That kind of dance is funny. You will see the men patrons cover their mouth in order to hide their laughter. Guys don't cover their mouths when they laugh, unless they're really embarrassed.

Blessing in Disguise

Your girlfriend's parents doesn't like you. They don't want her to marry you. So, you're getting the milk for free, all this time.

Robo-women

Your girlfriend is cultured. She likes broad way musicals, anything artistic, and eats gourmet foods. She sounds like a gay guy.

Bad Boy

I hope that her new boyfriend is an abusive pimp-like "a-hole." But then again, some women like that in a guy, so that she can be a victim.

Never

You don't tell a woman to shut-up. Talking is what they like to do.

Accounting

When you're dating single women, you put them in the accounts receivable column as far as sex goes.

The single mothers you date, are put in the accounts payable account.

Humanity

You're attracted to doctors. But, you won't follow that caretaker to a developing country.

Meaning

If a woman doesn't say I love you, first. Then, she doesn't love you.

Emotional

I didn't have many girlfriends. So when I see a woman crying, I assume that most women do that, and it's not a sign of mental illness.

Objectify

You describe women as being "hot."

Equation

1 + 1 (Attractive Woman plus High Maintenance) = Bitch

Bachelor

I can't get married because women will usually marry up in life.

Feminine Side

I will save myself for her. Is that a "chick" thing to do?

Ideal Man

Your parents want you to marry an Ivy league graduate. I have two words for them, "Milton Holt."

He is a local politician in Hawaii, who was a wife beater and crystal meth user. Tell your parents about that type of potential husband. I don't sound too angry and jealous when I lost her to his type.

Comfort Zone

You go for a woman who already has a boyfriend. This method has a built in excuse for not having a commitment to her. You would have a serious relationship with her, except for her darn boyfriend.

Impeachable Acts

We feel that we own President Clinton. We pay for his brains, and not his ass. Taxpayers aren't his pimp who controls his sex life.

Truthful

So, I'll give you a call in two weeks, unless someone better comes along in the meantime.

Stuck in the 70's

You're the same woman who gets excited by Peter Frampton's song, "I'm in You." Wait, is it you or me, who feels that way?

Natural

I will still love you even after your implants. You'll be the same person behind that bag of ocean.

Personal File

You asked your girlfriend how many boyfriends she had in her past. She will be like a contractor and give you a lower estimated number.

Stalker

It's a good thing that I'm shallow. A shallow person feels that stalking someone takes too much time.

Serious

Do you cuddle with her? Yes, then you're the boyfriend!

Indirect Question

When a guy ask her that she must have a lot of boyfriends as a compliment. That man really wants to know for his own information, and his chances when asking her out in the future.

Built-in Family

Am I going to have kids? Where am I going to find a hot single mother? It's hard to find one to fit this description.

Later

You don't call her until she's about to get married. Then you can say that, "see, you can't say I never called her back."

Not Lying

You checked on your canceled date by calling during that time period to see if she's home, and didn't make a lame excuse for canceling.

Conceited

It's rough for two beautiful people to be married. They always get their way all the time.

Catch Phrase

I have to stop falling in love with a person that I have sex with the other night.

Guarantee

If she has a pimp, I wonder if you can have sex with her for the right price.

Real World

Abstinence is like algebra. It's hard, and you don't use it.

Cultural Differences

That is not an obscene gesture, but a sign of love in another language.

First Love

You would think that your second obsession would get jealous of your first obsession.

Decision Incision

When you become an attractive women. Then I'll give you money.

Demographics

At what age, it's time to date a single mother in your dating pool.

Preference

You wanted her to say, "Oh my God," instead of "I love you."

Climate Control

If that's good sleeping weather, what's good sleeping together weather?

False Modesty

From the producers of "it's not you, it's me," comes the concept "of you're too good for me, and you'll make a good wife/husband for someone else."

New Term

He's a hetrophile because he likes to sleep around with the opposite gender.

No Vice

This is a small town where the massage therapists are legit while new age music plays in the background.

The sound of Yanni isn't very erotic while you're naked.

Olympic Event

Before you have sex, you have to blood dope yourself to last longer.

Peer Pressure Machismo

I don't know of any culture where guys admit that he loves her before a group of men.

Non-Threatening

They're a cute couple that even older people will smile at them.

Fact?

You're a woman. That makes you less of a man than me. I think.

Not Renting

They just got married. Is it a coincidence that they have the same address as before the wedding?

Guy Talk

How come when you guys get together? The word "p—" is said a lot of times.

Be Prepared

Why are you using a mouthwash? Are you planning to put your tongue where?

Fresh Scent

She smells as good as an unused prostitute.

Equal Pay

Women are generally paid 75% compared to how much men make. That difference of 25% is for dating money. This difference is also used for insurance of marriage, kids, and alimony.

Dream Man

Your breath was taken away when you saw a man with cigar and whiskey on his breath, have oily hair, and a vaseline covered face. "You like that in a man."

Imagination

Don't think of me when you use the bathroom or other disgusting things.

Name Calling

She is a slut because you don't own her.

Too Beautiful

You had a peek at that sight. That is considered stealing beauty.

Citizen Customer is Always Right

"I pay taxes" is no excuse for doing those things.

Share

I don't want to mix my laundry with his. The thought of his juices from his laundry mixed with mine, makes me nauseous.

Model

You have the perfect look for our local population. You should be the cover person on our phone book.

Schedule

You have to look in your TV guide in order to know if you'll be busy tonight.

Whipped

I can't do that. I have a wife. Whatever that means.

Talkin' Pimpin'

He is not the type to say, "I can't take those things, people will think I'm a gigolo."

Cause & Effect

Why do women suffer from mental illness? I think that they have husbands.

Insulted

He told me to choke my chicken. Do I smell like K.F.C.?

Physical Domination

I'm the man. I supposed to have the larger head.

Dumped

How many times did you hear, "I'm not your type" reason?

Correlated

Is your sex life and love life, the same thing?

Souvenir

What are you doing in a tourist shop? I know that you just want to look at the topless local girls postcards.

Not Manly

You're a guy. You don't say, "do you think I'm pretty?"

Invisible

How can I make her jealous when she doesn't see me anymore?

Image

It looks weird when your girlfriend's father has a ponytail.

Acting

How can you believe in those love stories in the movies when the actors are in love with themselves?

Drought

You consider a spit in your face as having French kissed with the exchanging of bodily fluids.

Scare

Just because you were turned down by them, you can't keep putting a hex on those people.

Fun

What kind of vacation do you take? The kind where your purpose is to learn different cultures, or is it to get laid.

Defense

It's rude when you penetrate.

No Initials Necessary

I'm a man. I have the luxury of listing my full name in the phone book.

Monk

What's the point of looking good if you're not going to get any action?

Beast

That kind of music doesn't go with a higher volume. What are you really doing hiding behind that noise?

Hang-out

I wouldn't loiter in front of an adult theme store. Is that "No Loitering" sign necessary?

Better Society

You won a humanitarian award for not having sex.

Created Equal

If we were nude. We still won't be wearing the same thing.

Conformity

Your parents want you to get married. That's a big hint, and a step to be like them.

Love Shack

When you're put out to pasture to stud. This is not a good environment to be in, because your wastes are lying around the place.

Remember

You were on top of her once, but it was in a yearbook's photo arranged in alphabetical order.

Motivation

He wasn't excited talking about that subject, but he was excited talking to you.

Cat Fight

I don't want to start a rivalry between you two, but she is prettier than you.

Multiple Personalities

I can't have sex when there's another person in my body. I don't believe in the double play.

Conversationalist

Do I need a sex organ if I don't use my voice box to socialize anyway.

Wrong or Right

If you can't tell your wife about this. The chances are that you're going to do something morally wrong.

Lack of Intensity

You don't have to go to a mental institution after that breakup. It wasn't that good.

Sinful

Don't describe that act as fornication. You make it sound like judgment sex.

Standing Proud

You can't pants that guy. He likes to show off the size of his thing anyway.

Contented

Those wives with their shorter hairstyles after marriage and then the even shorter after giving birth.

Feminism on Wheels

Do the ex-wives of motorcycle gang members sue their husbands for alimony?

Selfish

Double standards are all right if I come out with the better deal.

Find Yourself

Personal growth is to drift apart from each other.

Buy

How much do I owe for love? Does that include tax?

Fair Fighting

She's the right one if she doesn't use any sexual problem insults during arguments.

Sounds Like

What type of laughter does your girlfriend have when someone asks her if you're her boyfriend?

Same Thing

What's the difference between a good boy and a nice boy? It depends on where his politeness occurs.

He's a good boy to his own parents. He's a nice boy to the girlfriend's parents.

Cheap Sweets

You saved the rock hard candy from Christmas, and gave those to your girlfriend for Valentine's Day.

Just Friends

You acted like a jerk in order to leave. So, she has to call her real friend when her car stalls.

Storm of the Century

I thought that when hot meets cold, wetness would occur. This doesn't happen for humans.

No Hint

Does it work the same way for guys? When he says no, he means yes. When he says yes, he means yes.

Too Immature

People don't want to be around that person. He is too defensive. Everything you say to him, and he answers with, "you're disrespecting me!"

Another annoying person who can't win arguments and say, "you think you're better than me."

Fake Friends

We can still be friends if I don't have to spend money on you.

Sensitive Male

It's a play about a bunch of militia men talkin' about relationships.

Innuendo

"Insert your own sexist joke" is a sexist joke, because you said the word "insert."

Introvert

I walk alone. That's not the only thing I like to do alone.

Sales

You're an attractive woman. You'll probably have a "show the face" type of job.

Comedian

Do you trust a never married, or an ex-wives jokes type of guy?

Pathetic

I thought that desperation sounded sexy.

Loophole

If you self-love yourself. Is there such a thing as infidelity?

Understanding

Do you try to steal signals from women like how baseball coaches would try to steal the opponents signals?

Red Flag

Your new girlfriend has a past that involves a lot of lawsuits.

She talks stink about her rich ex-husbands. You do the math with her personality profile.

Enforcers

Businesses are hiring bouncers to stop sexual harassment at the workplace.

Gold-digger Paradise

Is "gold-digger" a sexist reference? His long time girlfriend is going to be his a wife after he wins the lottery or will acquire a large amount of money.

Be Prepared

You taped those romance movies. Those come in handy when you have a girlfriend. So, you can let her watch those tapes on the VCR while you can watch sports on the other television.

Favor

I can't marry you. Do you know that single women live longer? I'm not marrying you for your benefit, so that you can live to a ripe old age.

Soccer Mom

She looks like a private school kid's mother.

Make-up

You can tell the difference between a sex face or having sex face.

Feel Sorry

Your partner has a sad looking expressive face. So, people will think that you're being mean to her.

Art

A picture is worth a thousand words. I have a nude picture of you. I can think of a thousand right now.

Ignored

Would you put up with personal questions from her, if she isn't attractive?

Option

I can go steady with you, but I have someone on the side.

Call Screening

Since she had sex with me. I won't pick up the phone in the middle of the night, just to talk with her.

Receive

Only women can boink jerks because jerks are usually guys.

Small Man Complex

Men can say, "little woman I want to marry you," but can a woman say, "little man I want to marry you."

Environmentalist

You think that she is a hippie because she doesn't use perfume.

Cover Charge

What is the entrance fee for watching a live sex act? How about watching a live drug act? What kind of application forms do employers have at these kind of places?

Mail Order Bride

A lonely scientist will purchase a porn star's public hair to create his own clone of her.

No Solicitors

They come early Saturday morning. You're already mad because you didn't get laid on Friday night.

Less Effort

You pick up transsexuals because you think they're easy, and still more male than female.

Surveillance

You peeked on a voyeur's anonymous meeting.

Joke-Man

He's good at sexist jokes. I wonder why he doesn't have many dates.

Advertising

I can't figure out why showing cleavage goes with beer in those print ads.

Soap

A stink guy can get away with doing many things, except for getting laid.

Sissy Sport

F—ing is a man's sport!

What's My Motivation

Would guys fight with each other, if there were no women around to impress?

Background Check

Your girlfriend's parents have a database on you. The career you have, and the percentage of domestic abuse in that line of work.

401k

She considers him as an investment f—. She is looking for a potential maximum earner from a man.

Triple Crown

Is not thinking about sex or having sex, thinking of sex?

Silver

You don't want to come in second in the mind of your partner. Then, you can't have kids or your partner can't be in a sovereignty movement or be in the Jehovah's Witness.

Repellent

You're more attractive to other women if you have a girlfriend. The other way around when a woman has a lot of boyfriends. Guys doesn't want to smell another man on her.

The Rules

She follows "the rules." I know women like that. They're called ex-acquaintances.

Shame-Non Fiction Section

I can't get married. I have never kissed a girl in public before in my life. (True story)

Better Person

Where did you get the idea that men like challenges? If I could be president without any competition. I'll take it.

Non-Seller

Instead of a how to marry a millionaire guide, how about a book on marrying a penniless guy fresh off the boat.

Male Feminist

You have an excuse as to why you're not married. Marriage is the subjugation of women. Single women have the longest average life-span.

Wife Rules

Who controls the music at a wedding? That person controls the marriage. When did you hear heavy metal music at a wedding?

Safe House

You feel comfortable at strip joints and adult video places because you won't run into any ex-girlfriends there, as opposed to a supermarket.

More Chances

How many times do you apologize for being an a-hole?

Must-be Television

She has attractive women as friends. They must be filming a television show. Another reason might be that there's a gentlemen's club or a Barbizon class during lunch-time nearby.

Whatever Happen

When you mention her name, there is kind of a scared laugh reaction. Is she a psycho?

Makes Sense

What I hear is that she has a better boyfriend on the side.

Sanitary

Are these Kleenex for wiping tears, and not your love juice?

Take It On the Run

So, what if she's a sick f—! You're still getting some.

System

You can go out with different guys, and then weed out the ones you don't want. But, the men will fall in love with you. There is a chance that one of them will be an obsessive nut-case.

Equality

Why can't I call her tough-looking?

Guarantee

People will talk behind their backs when they see an old man with a young wife/girlfriend walking past.

Cute

I missed that episode of, "I missed you, you whore!"

Bragging Rights

If that person has flea infestation. Is it still "all good?"

Paging

I'm a guy. I don't need to control who calls.

Religious

He's a good boy because he is seen praying. But, do you know what he's praying for?

Complicated

The problem with sex is that there too much sex in it.

Choose

You like that person, but you want to keep your money. You buy your friendships.

Money Shot

You don't want to be treated by your looks. Then, why do you look in the mirror so often?

Questioning

If drinking and screwing are machismo. Why do women do those things too?

Boy Toys

The popularity of Pokemon will be a fad. So, it has to re-invent itself. How about an adult version called Taco Pokemon. You'll probably won't need a creative imagination to picture the adult version mascot.

Extinct

I haven't seen a Playboy since VCR's became common on the market.

Willpower

Guys can say no to sex. But, it has to be in a gay bar when he is a heterosexual, and sometimes when she has just finished with a Jenny Craig meeting.

Courtship

He has finally married that girl after a period of time. So, she must have finished high school then.

Income Priority

Who's the better man? Remember that the worst N.B.A player makes more than the best doctors.

Sad

You don't want to go out with a person with multiple personalities. because that means more people who will say no to you.

Dr. Love Dolittle

How do animals differentiate on which are the attractive ones?

In Common

When you and your girlfriend were watching a Lakers's game. You refer to Kobe Bryant as Kobe Tai Bryant as his nickname. Oh no, it was a Freudian slip with the use of a porn star. But, if your girlfriend know who she is. I think you found a good one.

Exotic

The kind of selection of adult videos are determined by the Hispanics porn stars who are located in the

Asian section.

Trade-ins

When you become a member of a born again religion. Do you exchange your literature of porn to a doom and gloom nature? Both sounds like the same type of reading to me.

Do It Yourself Editing

I don't think you should be a professional editor because you can guess which scenes are taped in slow-motion in a X-rated video. There are so many different scenes.

Social Awareness

You tell your fiancee that you can't buy a diamond ring because of the South African's thing.

Low

The worst insult he used on your girlfriend is that she is f—ing you!

Ideal Man

You aren't worried that this picture of your boyfriend. He is topless and carrying a semi-automatic weapon. (See Lee Harvey Oswald)

Bothering You

So, can I have your forwarding address?

Pervert

Why would anyone tear off the bathroom doors?

Depressed

You're not good enough for a woman, who would cry for you or love you back. One woman did, but since we didn't have sex, I didn't care about her.

Shopping

You went antiquing with your girlfriend. But, you thought that would include buying old baseball cards and X-rated videos made in the 1980's.

Revealed Future

Your girlfriend shouldn't talk stink about her mother. She will inherit the bad personality of her mom in a few years.

Translation

When your partner says she needs her space. It's the same thing as f-off.

A Guy Thing

Your dog is man's best friend. But, do you need to give him a penile implant as a form of friendship?

A Client and a Member

I thought that Minoxidil is supposed to stop middle age men from going postal.

Eliminates Excuses

"Sorry girls, he's not married!" She doesn't have an excuse not to go out with you in the future.

Down to Earth

You're too attractive and have a nice personality. You should be a bitch sometimes, in case a crazy guy wants to stalk you.

Different Rewards

A prize can't be sex when she's a woman. That's a reward for guys.

Matching Lips

When she says, "it's nothing." She will say this with a pouting expression.

Debate This

When you disagree with him, he takes off his shirt. The "show the body" argument is not in the debating handbook.

Beauty and the Beast

Would a beautiful woman fall in love with an abnormal looking guy living under the street? That story is a long way from women not making eye contact with even ordinary looking men on the street.

Money Talks

If she wants to get rid of him. The best method is for her to ask for non pay back loans and expensive gifts. She wins either way, whether he says yes or no to her suggestions.

Feel Sorry

I don't think he wants to hear, "you poor thing" when he is dumped.

Isolation

What's the purpose of being on a diet when she isolates herself? I thought that the purpose of being on a diet is to look good when other people can see you.

Okay, I Get It

She was with a group of other women. I saw her. She saw me. I approached her. She was certain that I would pick her. Then, she started to have a hacking cough seizure. I can take a hint. That's a no, huh!

Obvious Hint

"You're not grotesque looking!" Why don't women say this to me? This would make it much more easier on who to pick-up.

Franchise

Which type of drinking and eating establishments would have an ad that shows mammary glands?

Say

You told a woman with ball earrings, "I love you balls!" Are you happy that you said that stupid thing?

Understudy

You couldn't say, "I love you" to your girlfriend. So, you hired an actor to say it for you.

Right Nickname

You're called an ass-face because you put Preparation H around your eyes.

Possessive

You're cold and distant, but you become jealous when others showed friendship towards your friend.

Temptation Eyes

You're attracted to the snob look of the, "looking away with closed eyes" expression.

Keeping It Real

You check the shower drains to see if her hair color is real.

Master of Your Universe

Can you make a pass if you live in your own world?

First Impression

You look like the type to be used, and not the type to use people!

Permanent Scar

You can't have that back like your virginity, your soul, or your heart.

Helping Hand

That was thoughtful of the guy who fooled around with my wife, because he wanted our marriage to be more closer during a crisis.

Witness

Because you didn't see that part of the body. Don't assume that it's there!

Carnival Land Cruise

The kissing booth is supposed to be cute. I don't think it's cute for the spreading of viruses.

Say It With Feeling

There's a difference in the way you say, "what an ass, as opposed to whatta ass!"

Brain Thinking

You're brave enough to have piercing done to yourself. But, do you need more pricks on your body?

I can't control just one of them.

Capitalist Sisterhood

American women want to spread equality to women around the world. But, that just resulted in more competition from women coming here to America from cultural chauvinist countries.

Past Prime

Your girlfriend is an ex-model. I can hear the anger, mood swings, and the substance abuse already.

Category of What

I'm in the weird guy group. I'm not gay, and I have never had a steady girlfriend.

Bad Boy

I lost my girlfriend when she picked a guy with homicidal tendencies.

Turn-on and Turn-off

That guy who likes long walks on the beach is like a woman who enjoys paying for dinner dates.

Swear

Instead of saying "ass" all the time, you could say "poop shoot" in its place!

Ex-s

You have the same hopes for your ex-partners as in a high school reunion. You hope that she becomes fat, and he becomes bald.

Remote Control

You can't watch those programs after you get married!

Number One

What's better than sex? How about sex without infection.

Celibate

You don't have sex, so you're considered hetro-curious.

Needs Gouging

When sex is in limited supply, you can make it more expensive.

Miss Right

I think you found the right partner when she doesn't make a whining sound, after she doesn't get her way.

Conceited

He has the "me" style that only she could love. The rest of her family isn't thrilled with that style.

A Good Character

He hasn't been arrested for domestic abuse. Is that a rare quality for a man?

Search for the Perfect Woman

Your idea of perfection is that she uses a lot of makeup, chews gum, and has a cigarette going while spitting out something. She can do all of these things at the same time.

Stronger Gender

I don't know if men are weak. But, when there's a story about a strong woman. She is called a divorcee.

Hunters and Gatherers

A man has the ability to come back home empty handed after a shopping trip.

She's the One

One of your girlfriend's turn on is a stupid guy's laugh.

Dreaming

You will never hear your girlfriend use the word "sexy" to describe you.

Buffed

You're jealous of your girlfriend because she has a thicker neck than you.

Pretend

That is nasty! What is that phone number again!

Economy Size Matters

She looks like the type of woman who would drive a big family size car.

Stupid Fad

You can't streak if you expect to pick up women. The only people who will be chasing you. They'll have security written on their uniforms.

Speech Therapy

You lisp your pick up line of, "what's a wittle wady wike Woo?"

Danger Zone

You cut in line on someone's obsession.

Boo!

You scared her at first. Then, you asked her for a date.

Species

How can they be extinct? You mean that they can't adapt to changes. How hard is it to fornicate?

Marketing

Instead of Viagra, they should call it "Dick, don't fail me now!"

Afterwards

If you're pursuing a physical activity, why do you stop for a smoke?

Good Lover

It's a good sign when she says, "you like" during you know what.

Concentrate

You have to think hard, and use your two heads to beat as one for its purpose.

Melodrama

Opposites attracts, this only makes for television movies.

Chastity Belt

She has a natural birth control device with that annoying voice.

Sensual Smells

You can't be fruitful there because of the smell in the place.

Do Not Put In Washing Machines

The pants are so tight that you don't have pockets, or they are stretched out and stuck to your skin.

Three Degrees

The three degrees of being an a-hole are, plain a-hole, f-ing a hole, and sweet a-hole. Your advice is try to be in the third category.

Women's Sexuality

That's unknown territory for me. The closest thing that I can relate to, is the Q-tip in the ear.

Sequel

That's not an original sin. But, it's a remake of the same plot.

Magazine Smiles

You have to counteract your subscription to Hustler with a subscription to Psychology Today.

Confused

What to do? When a hysterical woman starts yelling at you.

Good Service

I know we can't talk prices. But, is there included a really big tip?

Socialize Sex

You want to take the profit motive out of sex, so that sex businesses wouldn't be sprouting all over the neighborhood. You'll get your voucher card on how many times you can have sex.

Co-op

I can't ask her to move into my place. This is a guy's place with a man's smell.

Studies

Pornography is tied to violence. Because it's usually a single guy who commits sex crimes. It can also be connected to the fast food take-out that's been the cause and effect for strange behavior.

Cholesterol All Over the Place

Which is more healthy for the community? A fast food place replaced a porn shop in the same location. I'll wait until the place airs out, and I can safely eat that special sauce.

Veggie Burger Substitute

If meat is murder. Did you murder your brains out?

Limited Choice

A man can't be picky, unless he has money.

Denial

His parents are suspicious because they think that she sleeps around on him. But, he will just say to that accusation, "not did I know of" in reference to knowing if she cheats.

Pimp

He's not an ordinary guy because he pays attention to her. He does that because he makes money off of her.

Shallow or Chew

Can you be serious with a person who dresses and have the same hairstyle as a celebrity in style?

Separation of Church and Sex

What religion are you? "Ah, s—, so I'm not getting any then. Okay, bye."

Exist

She's a nice girl. So, she probably doesn't know you.

Line

I wouldn’t do that even in the privacy of my home.

Lesson in Love

You mark the steps that you’re going to use in the future.

Different Situation

You replace the description of fast with the word “premature.”

Measurements

Those numbers sound like you have a good figure. But, the bad news is that it’s the measurements of your head.

Wrong Gender Myth

Your girlfriend has big feet. You mean that it’s not the same as for the guy with a high number shoe size.

Candid Camera

When an attractive woman approaches you. A guy will have to look around for any hidden camera. If he’s a guard. There are guys sneaking around in back of her. (warning) He can’t check her for wires.

Love Canal Scene

Lovers can’t frolic in acid rain. It’s bad for your skin and hair.

Apologize

That kind of moaning has "I'm sorry" thrown in at the same time.

Narrow It

When you say that you love woman. I think you should say that you love your wife.

Safe Sex

I thought that means that you look both ways before dropping your drawers.

Weakness

Don't laugh when I have thoughts of what a sensitive male would do in different situations.

Honey, I'm Not Home

I can't figure out the reason a wife of a great adventurer didn't go along on the trip too.

Evil

Will you tell that guy to stop with the womanizing smile?

Priorities

I can't figure out why your parents left the nude pictures alone, but tore up the articles on how costly a marriage will be, and how expensive is to raise a child.

Ratings System

I don't rate. I must be somewhere into a negative number.

Topless

He can't be half-naked. He is either all naked or not. He can be topless, which is considered clothed. But, when he is bottomless. He is considered totally nude.

Mind Your Manners

Will you stop saying "flaccid?" Would you want to hear that word coming from a doctor? That means you have a medical condition.

Bi-Curious

You married a bi-sexual person. The purpose of referring to oneself that way, is that she will probably cheat. So, you'll make your transition for a newer model that much easier.

Remember Me

You lost the argument when she couldn't remember your name, and you say that even strippers know your name.

Advantage

A good thing about being overweight is that it lessens your chances of being stalked.

Self-Promoting

She praised herself when she states that women are chasing after her instead of men chasing her, which isn't a difficult thing to happen.

High Definition

She's not a gold-digger, but someone who's counting on a guarantee lottery ticket.

All-Natural

Is it still considered going all natural when she has implants.

Human Spray

The smell of money is our version of cat-nip.

Blind Date

Which do you prefer to hear about her? She has a great personality, or she's just a manic depressive.

A Male Secretary of De-fensive

Will woman go out with you if you have a chick's kind of job?

Louder Attention

You can't cry to get your way when no one is around to see you.

Moot

You can have a lot of good points. But, if you're afraid of commitment. You're a jerk.

Differentiate

Your date night and your porn night are separate, but not equal.

Too Good to Be True

You can't trust a person who can make you feel good.

Don't Ask

Do you have children? Now, are they with the same woman?

We're Separated

She will have sex with another man for vengeance. His revenge is that he won't spend money on her, and the other woman will be getting things that she was supposed to receive.

Textbook

When their parents want to see them after being newlyweds. They want to see a baby. The questions are; what to do, and who will do it?

Parental Mindset

You have a girlfriend of the same race. Your mom is happy. When it's a she. Your dad is happy.

S— happens

I don't dump girlfriends. They just leave for some reason.

Salute to President's Day

He wanted to take the day off because of his break up with his hooker.

All Over the Place

You will need an attractive face in order for your genitals to look good too.

Fat Line Between Love and Hate

You don't have to kiss ass of a beautiful woman when you have no chance with her.

Life Is Not Fair

How can I compete with guys who wear muscle shirts? They attract all those nice girls in halter tops. There is no such thing as a bad hair day when you have a mullet hairstyle.

Pearls and a Long Dress

She's old fashioned when it comes to the having sex part.

X-chromosomes

I don't know whether to call her ma'am or a woman. She thinks that it sounds like she's old. She wants to be called a girl.

Changing of the Guard

I thought that women have children when their youthful sexual power fades. So, they have children for the purpose of having power over someone.

That's a Good Sign

When she doesn't confide in you, she doesn't think you're gay.

Best Friend Who Happens to Be a Girl

Is she going to bring her best friend to say the sassy or bitchy stuff?

Red Faced

She has passion. You mean that she becomes jealous. He has to lock his family jewels when he sleeps. A man who has passion and does that, and he's too controlling.

Smoke a Cigar

He shouldn't drink too much after the birth of his daughter. She might end up with a stripper's first name.

Offensive

You're a lesbian trapped in a man's body. So, when is your time of the month?

8 Track Tapes

You're in an age group where you date women who wear a scarf.

Pure

If you're attractive and poor, you must not be doing what men like.

Men in History

Your boyfriend will cheat and beat you. Luckily, our ancestors didn't do such things.

Open Your Ears

I said you have "broad shoulders" and not a 'broad's shoulders."

Amateur Producer

He will try to pick up a woman who lives at an earthquake fault line. He tempts her with moving in with him to a safe earthquake free area.

Don't Jump Off the Bridge

Terrible Billy Joe committed suicide. You could call that incident as terrible B.J., if there's such a thing.

T.O (Time Out)

An engagement ring is his way of buying time. Time is money, and marriage is money.

Daytime Talk

We don't categorize men on how sexually active they are. There are the ha, huh, oh yeah reactions to the number of women he slept with in his adult life.

Posters

The pictures of your girlfriend is taken from a telephoto lens.

Temptation

Is adultery wrong? What if the chick is hot?

A Man's Man

He's brave enough to wear a T-shirt with a strip club emblem out in public.

A Gun in His Pocket and Glad to See Him

Ricky lost a girlfriend to a guy who wears military camouflage pants.

Tight Fits the Mold

She wears dresses that shapes her ass. The dress will cover as much as a stripper before the money shot.

Dog Tags

Ricky doesn't know the name of the male dog in the neighborhood who comes around his female dog pet.

So, he will refer to that dog as her f— buddy.

Time-out Coach

Women will listen to a male when they're on a sports team even more than men will. But that doesn't happen in a marriage. It maybe has to do with the numbers of more than one.

For Your Crow Eyes Only

They should change the Bond Girls label to Older Woman Bond Co-stars. I thought political correctness are supposed to be for good and not evil.

Ms. Match

You would wrestle her, but she outweighs you by 100 lbs.

A Straight Line

You thought the shortest distance for a woman to money is through a rich man.

Reflections of

You remembered the yelling at each other years.

Sexual Ignorance is Bliss

You're comfortable when your parents have no clue when shown martial aids.

A Cup of Self-esteem

How can you live with that man? I know that you're smart and beautiful. So, how can you live with that man?

Uni-sex Bathroom

You're a sensitive young man. I can imagine your masculinity when you become older and slowly lose testosterone.

Hair on Back, Pimple on Ass

How can you cheer for a professional sports team filled with criminals? It's like cheering for the hairy guy in a porn movie.

A Drive-by Mansion

Chicks dig drug dealers, except for the gun play involved.

No Need to Ask

Is she hot? I know you wouldn't lift a finger if she wasn't attractive?

Low Interested Loan

You saw a beautiful woman driving a cheap car. Is she a grad student, on scholarship, or trying to make a honest living?

Not Adam and Eve, or Adam and Steve

I think it might have been Adam and Eva. The interpretation was a letter off in translation. Eva was created through the Russian bride web-site. She was ribbed for his pleasure.

Lawyers in Love

That male employer has mostly female employees. He has no sexually harassment charges. He must be socially conscience, or not successful in his business for a lawsuit.

Video Collection

The problem is that he likes to see the beautiful people "getting it" on tape.

Come Back for More

You keep going back to her. Does she work around alcohol, or oils and lotion?

Best Before This Date

Do you still think about your dream girl from high school? There's no expiration date.

No Looting

Don't be greedy! Have you taken enough of that seminal fluids?

One Sided Conversation

Do you talk to a woman with her arms crossed?

She's Got Eggs, She Knows How to Use Them

What's the point of having a genius male sperm donor when the offspring inherits their intelligence from the mother.

The Mask Avenger

Why do male vice cops wear a hooded ski mask to keep their identity secret? They want to keep this gig.

Where else can a man go "ha ha," and arrest a woman for taking money for sex?

Motivational Speaker

Guys will talk as much as a woman in a conversation with each other. She must have been attractive, or she's alone without any peer pressure around to give that "who is this guy" look.

Every Guy Has One

It is called an ego. You have a high opinion of yourself. My imaginary celebrity stalker is "The Facts of Life's Mindy Cohn." I don't think I'm alone here.

The Day After Explanation

She described him as a perfect gentleman. What does that mean? How long will he still date her when she expects him to be a perfect gentleman until marriage?

The Big "L"

He's one of those "leave my daughter and I'll give you money" type of male.

Scum-bag Territory

Any guy who posses the date rape drug. Not even Johnny Cochrane can make reasonable doubt explanations to erase his reputation.

Think Ahead

She picked a boyfriend who can scare her dad. Now, she has to live with that guy.

Opposite Directions

Some women will think that the more money he spends on her, the more he likes her. But some men will think that the less he spends on her and she's still with him, the more she likes him.

The Big House

It must be a coincidence that all the phone numbers from the women you picked up are 555-867-5309.

Below the Man Line

A guy who's a fan of boy bands, also thinks that John Gray has too much testosterone.

Get That, But it's Way Over There

Who thinks that men like the hunt? Why are there so many men living by a supermarket?

Sound Bites

Ricky was mislead into thinking that men pay to get off, and women get paid to get off.

What Are You Looking At?

That creepy guy doesn't mind the ringing cell phone because that's an excuse to look at someone. It's a letdown for him when an attractive person puts the cell phone on a vibrating ring. He can't stare at her.

The ringing bell in a movie theater is annoying because he can't see who it is.

Wardrobe Hint

She has to put on her "I have a boyfriend" clothes.

Trapped

Ricky thinks that he might be gay, so he has only has sex with money. So, there will be no emotional attachment.

I Will Survive

Ricky isn't married to this day because he has never danced in his life.

Virgin No-worries

If you worry about your image. You can't have sex anymore. There is a possibility of a hidden camera, even in the privacy of a bedroom. If you're a celebrity now or in the future. That videotape can be used as blackmail or become a product to be sold on the open market.

Genetic Make-up Hints

She might be out of luck, because she doesn't fit into any category of being a trophy wife. She isn't model like tall or thin, blonde, or Asian.

Safe Nerds

You can make fun of the virgin guy. But, they are the best dates for your daughter or sister.

Pretty Boy

When the guy is better looking than the girl. This situation works about as well as when the woman is taller than the man or when she makes more money than him.

Shoes Do the Talkin'

Platform shoes should come with an accessory sign of "I'm an insecure and easy person." Is it a coincidence that platform shoes is worn with slutty clothes?

Blind Date

I don't care about how physically attractive she might be. When she said that her best feature is her sarcastic wit. I'm there.

Her Benefit

When she has sex with a guy, he's going to exaggerate how physically attractive she is to other guys.

What guy brags about having sex with a woman with (code) nice personality?

Circle Date on Your Calendar

It's the third week of the month. A single guy will think that's the best time to go out because he thinks that's a week before women have their time of the month.

World Without Men

What is she talking about? She doesn't really need men now that there are turkey basters, if she wants to get pregnant. Who will apply the sperm? Maybe she's right, a straight guy will not touch or have anything to do with another guy's sperm.

She Shoots, He Scores

A woman having sex isn't an accomplishment. That's a male-oriented goal with obstacles.

The Match Game

Ricky has pictures of himself with different girlfriends. Can you match the girlfriend with how much money he was making at that time?

I Can Explain

Her excuse is to why she became pregnant is that "something must have gotten over her." I think that it was that something must have gotten into her.

Now You Say

It takes money to make money, and to say, "I love you."

Hurt a guy's feelings

Can you say to a guy? You're good enough to f—, but not good enough to marry.

Male Fraud Friends

It's funny how her male friends are attractive. She wants a relief pitcher who has the potential to reach home plate.

I Believe

She will hint to Ricky that she receives expensive gifts, but she's better than a gold-digger because she will accept less expensive ones.

Squat Lifts

That's a whole episode. She has a man's ass.

Rich Sweet Glands

A "no fat guys" t-shirt would be effective if she wasn't attracted to his high living lifestyle.

Self-Deprecating Abuse

This material could be considered a jerk-off book. No, you don't jerk-off because of its sexual content.

The author of this book is a jerk-off.

Valentine's Day Massacre

Do you hold back laughter when you see a guy who wears a matching red shirt with his wife or girlfriend?

The letter "W" on the shirt could stand for "wussy." I don't believe him when he said that the big red "W" stands for the University of Wisconsin.

Should men really complain about Valentine's day? A woman probably has a 20 year span of receiving stuff from age 16 to about 36. That's when there's an expiration year for Valentine's day.

Not Married in the U.S.A

A man can make money in this country by marrying a foreigner who wants to be a citizen of the U.S.A.

That's a guy's version of when marriage pays off in his mind.

You Can Do Better

Ricky had an ex-girlfriend who married a rich man. He must not be too rich because he would have married a younger trophy wife.

Sadly Hawkins Day

The only women Ricky can think of who face rejection are of the old strippers trying to find work.

Hero Comes with Assets

She's in the service (non-sexual) field. So, she doesn't have an "I don't need a man" kind of occupation.

Enjoy Your Meal

Will she be good in bed if she considers anything other than intercourse as freaky?

Social Conscience vs. Materialism

Ricky is debating with himself if he wants to buy his fiancé a diamond ring. Because he doesn't want to contribute to white ruled South Africa. (I ain't going play Sun City. Apartheid!)

Skin Deep

She could look like an actress, if it wasn't for the drug use that has done to her face.

Dating Last Words

Ricky knows when to cut his losses. The last he sees of her is when she says, “I’m not a cheap girl.”

Sexcise Tax

The younger women are more expensive because of the tack on shipping costs attached to the maintenance fee.

Disturbing Behavior

There’s a high rate of AIDS in the developing countries. So now, where will rich guys be able to go to have sex with underage girls when they travel abroad?

Gullible Travels

Beautiful, Virginal women will greet you in the hereafter when you die for a cause. My question is, “Are they shaved or unshaved, I mean their underarms.”

The Backdoor Boys

So, If you like anal sex, it won’t be an insult when you’re called an a-hole.

Tasteless Tails

Why do men have money? So, women will talk to them. Wait, talk isn’t the word. What’s that word?

Not Starving for Attention

Your date had quite an appetite for a first date. You might want to check his/her parents about the metabolism gene.

Time-Line

Ricky hasn't been or believed in love since Spandu Ballet was popular.

Assoul Mate

A person can only dream about having a partner who says, "why don't you make more money."

Hostile-Ranting from a Madman

Why do I sound so angry? I don't think it has to do with being a guy who hasn't gotten laid in 10 years.

Conclusion

Why don't I have a steady girlfriend? I blame this on the higher ratio of men to women here in Hawaii.

OBLIGATORY CHAPTER

Welcome to the Intolerant Show

When guys are alone. Do they make sure that their statements are politically correct? Seinfeld used the "not there's anything wrong with that," to get away with having homophobia jokes. If there are no women around, or a camera recording what men say in private. They don't have to watch what they say.

Lesbians-Ricky's Take

Lesbianism is like Communism. It looks good on paper, but it's not financially viable.

You would think women would go to gay bars for the conversation, except they would have to buy their own drinks.

I think I'm shallow. Whenever there are lesbians on television and they're not attractive. The remote control goes click to another channel.

I think I know why there aren't lesbians hostess bars. Because it's hard to con a woman with sex as a dangling carrot.

Ellen Degeneras has modify her classic phone call to God bit with asking him if he can recommend some hot girl-girl videos. An actress's agent might worry about her marketability if she's described as a prettier Ellen Degeneras and its insinuation.

You're a male rock groupie, and you follow the Indigo Girls.

She didn't receive alimony from a rich man who had an affair. It can only mean that she is a lesbian.

Your favorite college team in women sports is the Lady Anteaters. Who is their mascot? I think it might be K.D. Lang.

The comedian fake the joke when he didn't use a lesbian reference when talking about a radical feminist.

Your grandmother was a consultant with the Dick Vandykes show.

Machismo

Ricky doesn't understand when a guy calls him a "pussy" as an insult to his manhood. "Pussy" might just be the most powerful thing on the planet.

Another attempt at an insult is, "I'm going to make you my bitch." Geez, I think you just insulted yourself because the both of them will be participants in that act.

You're a man. How do you know if he snores in bed? Explain yourself!

Ricky's Homophobia

You suffer from hypertension. I think you should be taking low sodium condoms.

When Elton John sings, "Don't Let the Sun Go Down on Me." You say, "all right, instead how about your daughter then."

Straight guys are angry at gay men because there is the impression that the sex is cheap. Guys hate that you can pick up a partner at a public park and spend next to nothing. There aren't many gay nudie bars, because the competition is public bathrooms.

I need a female chaperon at a bus stop that is located in front of a gay bar. My friends might see me there and get the wrong idea.

You questioned your friend's masculinity when his major is of a foreign language.

My parents might think I'm too feminine if I cut my own hair. I will make sure that's is a little crooked.

Having an enema leads to homosexuality.

In a car with other guys, the reason you gave when you were in an accident. You were distracted by an attractive girl on the street.

When your parents found your collection of porn and didn't object, because it was of a heterosexual variety.

You defended the banned gay teacher because who's going to teach you how to dance.

You don't care if the animal you just ate was of a male or a female variety.

You think it's funny when two guys say good night to each other.

You're so naïve that you thought that going to a cockfight is flirting.

Your pet bull went gay, and you thought that it must be its upbringing.

You belong to a group banning abortion for homosexual parents.

You're glad that you weren't breast fed as a baby because you had gay male parents.

You become defensive when you say, "I said I'm home, not I'm a homo." (in an accent)

You wonder why he keeps winning on the bets on which guy can stay away from women the longest.

You watch old school television, and you believe the premise that Gomer Pyle has a girlfriend.

You go cruising, complete with a handle bar mustache. (late 70's time-warp)

You look good enough in drag to give a ride to your city's red light district.

You were voted as part of the cutest couple at an all boy's school.

I applaud your work with ACTUP.

I don't stare at women, but there are gay people around, so I hope they can take the hint.

A love song is written by your articulate boyfriend.

There's an innuendo when you have a fight with a male dancer.

The silly grin you have when you hear Mrs. Michael Jackson, Mrs. Richard Simmons, and Mrs. Janet Reno.

If girls matured ahead of boys by three years. How much is it for gays to mature faster?

What was the gay club in high school? It must have been under the what club.

You can't carry your books to your chest. This was before the backpack became popular.

You're worried that you're attracted to women in three piece suits.

The sex business ads are in the sports section, but there aren't any gay or bi-curious ads included.

You have to look both ways before you kiss a picture of a guy.

You watch movies for "that's so gay scenes. Also, you can't watch a movie with Tom Cruise or Brad Pitt in it because of your gay tendencies.

N.C.A.A.

No C—k at All! (For Women) No C—t at All! (For Men)

A disadvantage of being gay in high school is that you can't be a jerk. High school is supposed to be your being a jerk years.

A heterosexual guy's diet is to watch gay porno after dinner.

Your well meaning parents put an ad in the newspaper with your picture, and the line of "help cure this boy to be a real man."

Your bi-sexual accountant calculates the cost of having to spend on having sex with male as opposed to a female.

You're a gay guy. Do you care what the other guy does for a living?

At what age, you didn't have a gay experience. You can be considered not gay.

You only have lunch dates and not dinner dates with a woman. Are you married or gay?

Urban Legend

They'll kill your women, and rape your men.

Sports-break

Ricky can't watch or listen to a sportscaster who uses the term "rimming" on a missed basketball shot.

Network sportscasters won't make gay jokes even when they do shtick. Some sports lingo are set-up for gay references, but they'll stop themselves from making them.

A sportscaster won't say that this play will suck the opponent dry.

A reason why the networks don't want gay jokes during a sporting event is because kids may be watching.

You haven't been around a playground where boys throw around the f-word (rhymes with tag) like there's no other words in their vocabulary.

Show Biz

Who's gay in Hollywood? Wouldn't it be easier to name, who's not gay in Hollywood? Uh, there's Jack Nicholson, Charlie Sheen, and that's about it.

Odd Couple

They're professional roommates, he's a doctor, and he's a lawyer. You're not fooling anyone.

Don't Turn Around

You know that the male director is probably gay because the actors are better looking than the actresses.

Wall to Wall Coverage

Is there an area on you that no man has gone before?

Padded

You look away real fast when you stared at your own gender for a longer period of time then you're comfortable with yourself.

Infantile

You're glad you weren't breast feed, because you were raised by a gay couple. It might have improved your sucking power.

The Better Man

You're challenged to a one on one contest because he wanted to shower with you after the game.

Psycho

You remembered as a kid when a bully called you a fag. You chased him with scissors, and try to cut his hair. That action suspended you for a week, but it gave you a reputation a kid who took homophobia to the max.

Anal Retentive

You volunteer to have a computer chip up your bum, courtesy of a government survey.

Ballerina

You're a man who wears a leotard top, but when he leans over, he looks like he has breasts.

Beard

She's my fake girlfriend, but not in a Mrs. Rock Hudson sort of way.

After You, Please

You offer him to go ahead in line, because you don't want him to be in back of you.

No Win Situation

When a feminine voice guy insults you, the only response you can do, is to shrug your shoulders.

Uncertainty

I'm scared to ask that macho guy if he's gay, because I'm going to be riding with him alone in his car.

The Non-gay Gene

You have a quick gag reflex. That means what I think you can't do.

Watch Your Manners

You can't swear in mixed company, so you don f— in mixed company too.

The Missing Episode

I want to get hold of the, "guess what, I'm a man," episode of Star Trek. Capt. Kirk can't be completely certain of the genders from different alien life forms.

The Real Scared Straight

How many guys won't commit crimes because of the fear of being raped in prison thing?

Sorry, I Gotta Go

A man with a cartoon voice asked you for a b.j in the red light district.

Don't Stare

How long will you look at each other in a dressing room gym?

The Humor Gene

No matter how liberal I think I am, I still have to hold back giggling when I see a same sex couple holding hands.

You're Not Then

You had your chance to come out as a Gay Asian male after seeing "The Wedding Banquet." If a good movie can't inspire a person to make an announcement of what you are. You have nothing to worry about those non-existing unanswered questions.

Name Change

His name is Rex. He might be heterosexual, but with name of Rex. He is thought to be gay for pay.

You're Listening to the W.N.B.A

The W.N.B.A is where a lesbian groupie has to pay the athlete, because sisters don't receive the same amount of money for the same amount of work as a man.

Know the Percentage Beforehand

That smell expert believed that he can smell if a stripper is a lesbian. He has a 9 out of 10 chance to be correct. It would be tougher to point out the 1 out of 10 who is not a lesbian.

Gay Town

You live in a community with a high cost of living, but there are a lack of attractive women who would flock to an area with rich guys.

Star-billing

Who's the star of a gay wedding? With two grooms, there are only co-stars. Who will tell which bride is a bigger star at a lesbian wedding?

Have Love Appraised

Do lesbians buy expensive engagement rings?

Men don't Grow on Trees

Is she really a lesbian? The first thought she has is that she doesn't need a man because she can make her own money.

Flannel Shirt

She isn't considered "alternative" if she shaves her armpits.

Fag Hag

She is the "before" she became the elderly lady with lots of cats.

Movie Advice

You just might want to stay away from a movie where there's a line that goes, "—dat Ass!"

The Good, The Bad, The Ugly

There's nothing funny about a man's ass.

The Gay Agenda

That's scary stuff. I remember when I had to look side to side for impending danger. Now, I have to also check from behind.

Boys Don't Cry

That person is having a sexual identity crisis. It's a good idea to hang around with morons.

Gay-dar

He has to put his "gay face" on.

Stop Beating Around the Bush

If you could make him do that. You will make a certain community happy.

Hint of Tolerance

I never received a gift from a girl in high school. But, I did receive a present from a gay classmate.

Go Straight to Hell

I don't want to see same gender marriage.

I mean, what's next.

What if a man wants to marry his pet dog for a tax break.

I can see it now.

You're at a business party, and you introduce your partner to the boss.

"Mr. Johnson, I like you to meet my wife, Fluffy."

That will help you move up the corporate ladder.

You can't be president.

Imagine at the Inaugural

"Ladies & Gentlemen, the president and the first lady of The United States."

(Hey, there's a bitch on the tube)

"What?"

"Look, that bitch on television!" (Barking dog sound can be heard in the background)

This message is brought to you by Peepers Inc.

NOT AN "A" STUDENT

Why do you have to be called Asian-American? Can't you be just plain American without the slash American label. You know, Dave works here and he's just like us. Who is Dave? Don't you know who he is? He's the Japanese guy in Accounting.

Asian Family Structure

The structure is similar to the game of chess. Dad is the king. Mom is the queen who controls the board in the family.

Ricky's Parents

Asian parents are not physically domineering. So, how can they have discipline from their children.

These proprietors of obedience become cute when they get older. So, their kids don't want to be seen as a bully when they're around fragile elderly people.

When my parents don't know something, there is pressure that I have to know the answer. That is why I'm going to school. I will have to know the textbook answers to any problems.

Growing Up of Asian Ancestry

Ricky believed the myth that the more slant in your eyelids, the smarter you will be. He has rounder eyes. Ricky was the

dumbest guy in the smart class, but the smartest in the dumb class. His classes with the
school's intelligent students didn't help his G.P.A.

Ricky wasn't popular in high school. Because looking older was cooler in that setting. Younger looking people are supposed do better later in life.

If you're Asian and popular in high school because of your looks, chances are that you won't be winning any academic awards. Good looks can make you a slacker.

You're not Asian when school is going to be fun.

I'm not supposed to have a girlfriend in high school. That rule of thumb didn't make any difference as to why I didn't have any girlfriends.

Your hairstyle can be considered a disgrace to the family.

The Joy Luck Weigh-in

She would be Americanized when her mother will nag to her daughter about her weight.

In high school, where the Asians are nerdy and the whites are gawky. They're our future bosses.

JAP- (Japanese American Princess) You're a daughter of professional parents.

Why aren't you in the smart class when you're Asian? Is there something wrong with you?

The look of fear on my face when a group of Asian teenagers are loitering around the classroom after the science club meeting. I have to walk the other way and not run into them ruffians.

You grew up with the expensive clear soap in the bathroom, which you're not supposed to use. Don't play with your guy friends after using that soap, because you don't smell like a boy.

In a Non-speaking Role

When a television show has a scene in an Asian town, which is located in an urban city. I look for Asian faces in the background and wonder. They choose a career as being walk-on actors. What will their parents think about that choice of profession?

Talkin'

Ricky has the shyness of a local guy. We speak in a "mumble, mumble" manner. This isn't a skill you want to have if you want to go into a field of public speaking.

Two Wongs Make a Right

You would think that a local guy name Wong wouldn't be so tall. In Hawaii, he's probably of mixed race, because the kid is over 6 feet tall.

Tone Loud

Is your Asian girlfriend a smoker or a Korean? Unfortunately, the transition from speaking Korean into English makes it sound as if you're scolding the person in which you're engaged in conversation. That causes a misunderstanding with Korean grocers who seem as if they're yelling at you.

Patronizing

Ricky had a Chinese ex-girlfriend. He just wanted to make her mad at him, so that she could yell at him in Chinese. No matter what she yells, it still sounds cute.

Sporting Looks

I know it's tradition. But, do they still have to have that Gavin MacLoud look?

Thespian

As an Asian actor, you're no Sammo Hung. He is the Nicholson of Asian actors.

Old School

My grandfather knew only one phrase in English. It was "son of a bitch" when I played in his garden.

Sense of Identity

As a child, the only Asian kid I saw on television was the Japanese boy who had his cap on sideways, short pants, and yelled to Godzilla.

A Country Puts On Its Best Face (The Old Bait and Switch)

I watch the Korean television station, because when I click the remote. I see a Korean actress, and think that all Korean women look like those actresses. The same thing happens on American television when people from other countries see our actresses such as Julia Roberts and think all American women look like her.

You Like Fight

Ricky has the local mumble accent style of speaking. It goes back to a cultural influences of being humble.

As a kid, when a local guy tries to speak in a proper English manner. He will get his ass kicked by the other local boys.

Local Slang

Whatever they say on the mainland. We just shorten that phrase. Sometimes, a person who isn't familiar with pidgin. They will hear just syllables and try to figure what's been said.

Timeless Fashion

You have an "Aloha shirt" dad.

Too Conservative Parents

They won't let you hang a poster of Bruce Lee in your room, because he is shirtless.

European Influence

When Asian women streak their hair with blond streaks or have eye jobs. This is a form of insecurity for wanting a westernized look. A myth might occur from their insecurity. They might have a reputation for being good at giving a good Lewinski (spelled with an i instead of a y) for a more ethnic touch.

You might want to try the Lewinski til completion or a Lewinski's Happy Ending.

Contradictions

I'm trying to figure out how communism exists in China where you can't use a natural for business mind.

Yo Mama-San

You won't yell "banzai" at weddings, because it's displays fascism towards the mother country.

You Won't Root, Root For the Home Country!

The California universities and the University of Hawaii have similar percentage of students in regards to ethnicity. But, when I see a mainland college cheer-leading squad, I see a token Asian female. Hawaii has their cheer-leading squad comprise mostly of Asian females. This might be because the spectators at an U.H. game are of Asian ancestry, so there is a kind of comfort zone for her.

Not Fair

An Asian face is rarely on the People's list and other surveys of the most beautiful women, because mainstream American women won't vote for an Asian woman. Because they win the American male's fantasies surveys in those sex magazines.

They Sure Stick Together

Asians only like to hang around their own kind. No wonder, there were the Korean and Vietnam wars.

Who Waste Money

As a kid, when you go to an English speaking movie with your immigrants' parents. You worry that they
will sleep in the movie theater.

Patronize/Americans-dominate Gene Color

It doesn't work when you make bimbo Asian women jokes. It will work better when you use a "being too cute" kind of jokes.

Non-B.M.O.C (Big Man on Campus)

In high school, a place where the Asians are nerdy and the whites are gawky. The B.M.O.C make up our prison population. They like the small enclosed space with its own "fists rule" society.

Can Be Done

The greatest professional football coach used pidgin in his teachings. There's a commercial on E.S.P.N where Vince Lombardi at the chalkboard diagrams a play and states, "with a seal hea, a seal hea" in a New York accent.

Aw, That's Cute

She's an Asian-American woman, so where's the picture of her as a little girl in a kimono.

Buddy

An Asian male will have no problem having a white guy friend if he has a sister. An Asian guy wouldn't scare him like a brother of color would. But, there's the one white guy friend who wants to be more than friends.

Silly

He likes Asian women with big breasts. (real or augmented) How long has he been attracted to sumo wrestlers?

Window to Your Ancestral Soul

You can't try to guess which Asian nationality that person is, behind those sunglasses.

Our House

Ricky's parents did a fine job of remaining humble. He lived in a middle class environment. But, when he saw the homes of some his snobbish classmates. Their homes weren't that big in comparison

Never Left the Island

"From coast to coast" to a residence of Oahu is from Makaha to Hawaii Kai.

WRAPPED AROUND A TWINKIE

Family Picture

A local Asian family portrait has the token white guy in it. He is affectionately called Waldo. He is the guy who got into the picture by marriage, and he has to crouch down in order to be seen. He can only be in the picture when another sibling married another Asian ancestry person before their marriage.

Someone of the offspring has to cover the full Asian coupling to meet the family obligation.

Local Asian Marriage

You're going to marry another Asian person. Are you worried that you might not receive an inheritance, if you married someone of another race? Your parents are still old school with a plantation mentality.

They remembered the times when they were looked down upon by their so-called superiors. So, they wouldn't like it much when they worked so hard all their lives. Then after they passed away, the land goes back to the racial group who were their bosses from the old days.

Madame Dragon

Asian women have an opportunity to be the boss in hostess bar/strip joint businesses. They finally have a chance to boss around those white dancers at these places.

The Marriage Word

There seem to be a lot of single local men out there. It's not the fault of the local women here, but it takes a gun to his head to make a local guy get married.

Role Model

Ling of "Ally McBeal" is considered a role model for young Asian American women. She is the before picture of a mama-San at a hostess bar. The photograph of a mama-San in those newspaper ads is those taken in the 1960's, where she has the Mary Tyler Moore's mod hairstyle.

Media

"Me love you long time" is the stereotype image of the submissive Asian women that American males like. No Asian woman has ever said that to me. I don't look American enough for her, so I think they're being themselves with me.

In Demand

Asian-American women won't call you back. It's not that they are passive, but they're the ideal women now in an era of strong feminism. So, they can be picky and choose the best of the lot of eligible men.

Asian Women / White Men

Asian women dating white men are the norm these days. So, when a white man sees an Asian woman dating a non-white male. The white man will say "hey, he's dating our women." He's been living in Hawaii too long that he might have forgotten that he is a white guy.

Some white men will date an Asian woman because there're insecurities of her physical traits such as height and having rounder eyes. Asian culture emphasize lighter color skin as being more attractive. How often would a white man wish to be black or Asian? (This doesn't include a temporary wish to be black when singing, dancing, or playing sports, or to be Asian just before taking a math test.) An Asian guy would jump at the chance to be white permanently. A white guy can put all those insecurities along with the self-esteem of a woman in a patriarch society, and he's got it made.

It's no coincidence that the White Male/Asian Female happens most frequent of interracial couples. They match economically, socially, physically, and looks right when walking side by side. An Asian Male/White Female couple has that Tom Cruise and Nicole Kidman height comparison when they're side by side.

Asian Male/ White Women

You don't see dating between Asian males and white women, unless it's those Waikiki, "Hey, you wanna date" kind of women you meet on the street.

She is a white woman in a short skirt and high heels who can speak better Japanese than a local guy.

He saves his date money for those high priced blond girls that is done in discreet privacy. He has a platonic local Japanese girlfriend for show to their parents, so she can be with her white boyfriend on the side.

Same

You dated white women? What's it like? Let me explain. When you date white girls, just think of the male version. They have basically the same characteristics. That goes for all racial groups too, where the males and females of an ethnic group have the same basic qualities.

Asianphile

Ricky thought that white women in college who majored in an Asian language or Asian studies, would date Asian guys. But, if she was into Asian men. She is in the wrong department. She should be in the Engineering department.

White on White

White couples in Hawaii have something in common. The guy probably has a tattoo. I don't know if having a tattoo gives the impression that he is a skinhead. But, if he has an Asian girlfriend. She would have an objection from her parents about his personal appearance.

Genocide

Asian parents can't be paranoid that whites would like to get rid of all Asians. Asian cuisine is too tasty to be without those type of restaurants in the world. Also, white men like Asian women too much for the genocide of all Asians.

Not Jealous

Ricky tried to make local girls jealous by trying to date non-Asian girls. It didn't work because they could care less, and guys are always coming on to them.

Myth

Once you go Asian, you never go back. That only works when you're an Asian woman. For Asian guys, you're in demand in a gay community.

The "once you go something, you never go back" myth can be turned into a sexist statement by adding. She will never go back when he stops supporting her in a way that she has become accustomed.

Fetish

You want to meet a Chinese woman. You have to attend a university. But, if you want to get laid, you have to go to one of those money up front places. The women at these establishments share the same characteristics of being smart and nice with the educated ones.

3 Strikes

A white guy has three obstacles he runs into when he wants to marry an Asian woman. The first obstacle is that her mother has to deal with a white mother in law. She still has an inferiority complex towards a white lady. She doesn't want to lose her matriarchal power within an Asian family. The mother in law relationship can work, if they don't live in the same area. They don't have to invite each other to family functions because of the distance. The second obstacle is that her father will probably be half the size of her white boyfriend. The father will want to intimidate the future son in law, but the difference in physical statue makes it impossible. The third obstacle is that the parents of both sides will have the ego thing where they want their kids to look like them.

Desirable

You're lucky when you're a white male. Since, you're the most desired by women of all races. He can get away with being an a-hole. Non-white males have no margin of error with any rude behavior.

Difference

When an Asian couple decide to get a divorce, the parents will say, "why can't you two get back together?" But in an interracial marriage, their parents will say, "well, that happens!"

Favorite

You like that actress because she is of your racial background, and she has a boyfriend of the same race, so it doesn't hurt your insecurity.

Travel Bride

I want to compare the difference of the numbers when an American man goes to Asia and comes back with a wife, as compared to when he goes to Europe and comes back with a wife.

Red Flag

You believed the stereotype of the submissive Asian woman, so that a twice divorced Asian woman puts a scare into you. You don't want to take your chances on a person who went against a positive stereotype.

American Top 40

Ricky can't marry an Asian woman instead of an Asian-American woman, because he was brought up in the American pop culture. It would be easier for him to have conversations with a person having similar references in their background.

A Good Man

It's hard for a woman to keep a successful husband. When he's white, he trades up for a younger model, and when he's Asian, he has a mistress.

Patience

When you're an Asian/American male who wants to marry an Asian female, you will have to wait till she is dumped by her first true love. She will be older and more cynical now, so you'll have a typical neurotic American woman, and there's nothing wrong with that, if you can handle it.

Universal

If you're looking for the perfect woman who will be attractive and submissive. Your search will take awhile. When she knows that she is physically beautiful, no one tells her what to do.

Bourgeois Relationship

Some men wouldn't mind paying for dinner dates when he knows that she is a traditional woman. She doesn't sway back and forth of a modern woman with its little perks.

Didn't Buy

An Asian mother won't believe her unmarried daughter when she says that there are no available men out there. Just a few calls, and she'll have her on a blind date before the weekend.

Manifest Destiny

You're in the dominant race, when even the fat guys of that racial background can marry the beautiful woman in the lower economical scale.

Not Lucy and Ricky

There is a superiority on how well you speak English in America. The relationship between a husband and wife will be easier when the husband doesn't have a thick accent. When the wife has a heavy accent, she doesn't have the dominant role. This situation is similar to when a wife has a higher income than the husband. Exception to the rule is, if he's Antonio Banderas or a Latin lover.

Men Are the Romantic One

Your girlfriend is the practical one in the relationship. Your Asian girlfriend is the practical 2 square in the relationship.

Too Shy

The men who go to a Bon Dance are white guys who want to pick up Japanese girls when learning to speak Japanese is too difficult.

It's Not the Weather

Which will have more straight white males leave Hawaii? Hawaii becomes a sovereign state or a law which prohibit any interracial dating or marriage.

Must See TV

African/American women want to see more successful African/American men date white women on television. (O.J. Simpson was acquitted to be a poster child for interracial marriage out of a Bob Jones F-University way of thinking.) White women want to see more romance between White males and Asian women in movies. (Whatever happen to Ross's Chinese girlfriend on "Friends"?) Single straight males want to see more emotional lesbian relationships that aren't in a porn movie. (You're hoping to see some sugar walls.)

Anna & Who's the King

Asian leading men in the movies should be asexual. Because an Asian guy in America don't want those insecure white men having the same fear they have about those threatening leading Black men.

Too Many Letters

An Asian/American married woman has a hyphenated with two Asian last names. It's a coded announcement to the older generation of Asian/Americans that she married someone of the same race.

Nip & Tuck

I don't remember her as being Eurasian. But, she is going to have that "to look like a white girl" surgery.

I Have My Answer-Local Call

He won't ask her if she has a boyfriend because it sounds too forward. So, he will ask her if her boyfriend is of the same ethnicity. He's hoping to hear that she doesn't have a boyfriend. If she tells him about her boyfriend. He will look at his watch, and say that he has to go.

American Gigolo

When you see an Asian/American woman driving around with a good looking non-Asian male in the passenger seat. I wonder if she's paying the bills.

Waikiki Hustler

These playboys hope for a strong Southeast Asia economy, so that Asian office girls will vacation in Hawaii, and be their male escorts around the island.

Smile On Camera Three

He's able to keep an appearance of tolerance of a male host on a dating game show when there's an inter-racial couple where he's the same race as the woman contestant. He will make jokes like a class clown would say to the popular guy in school in order to look cool.

Social Insecurity

How do you handle a sexual braggart? You can play with his mind, and ask him if his girlfriend still dates black men.

Soldiers Keep Coming and Coming, Not Coming, and Coming

Ricky heard that a hippie socialist from the 1960's theorized that the Vietnam War happened because America's repressed sexuality. Then, we should be watching out for Communist China with its high male to female ratio. They're a ticking time-bomb. Unless the male population turns gay, there will be a lot of frustrated and angry Chinese guys out there. (So, all you women out there, you better give it up to a Chinese guy or someone that looks like one. Then there won't be a WWIII.) Signed by an American Asian male who wants to get laid.

Chicks Dig The Attitude

A not so good looking white male can hit on an attractive woman and feel as if he has a chance with her. But not even a handsome Asian guy will try to pick up a pretty woman because he feels he doesn't have a chance with her.

Sweat Shop Dating

It could be a coincidence that his girlfriends have all come from developing countries.

Neck Exercise

Ricky remembered when he used to double-take when seeing an interracial couple. Now, he double-takes when he sees an attractive Asian woman with an Asian male. He can't figure out why she isn't with a white man.

Media Engineers

Ricky can't blame the Hollywood's male suits who cast the interracial relationships between an Asian and a white being of a White man and an Asian woman in movies or television. They're usually a young couple. They don't cast an older interracial couple. It's not sexy, and probably show them in a comical manner. Ricky watches Asian television drama programs. He doesn't remember seeing an interracial romance. That non-existence of life there doesn't reflect what happens in the Far East. Asian men control their media there.

Asian American males might not like to see the casting of a white actor as the love interest for a Lucy Liu or a Tia Carrere. There was an answer with an Asian male and White female couple with the casting of Pat Morita and Cloris Leachman. A straight white male would feel threaten to see Cloris Leachman in the arms of an actor of another race.

The Non-Show Off

There must be rich older Asian males out there. How come you don't see him with a trophy wife in public? His mother must still be living and won't allow it. If he is seen with a young woman of another race on his arm in the U.S. He will probably be hate crimed.

No More Voting Blocks

Who would object to an Asian/White marriage in Hawaii? Possible groups might include cosmetic eyelid surgeons or Hawaii's Democratic party. Unfortunately, tolerance contributed to the current political power of the Hawaiians as a racial group.

A Good Sign?

She is hassled by guys of her own race because she dates outside of their race. This means that she is attractive because guys wouldn't care if she's not pretty.

Weasel Days

That bugger will look for women of the same race who just had a breakup with a guy of another race. He will make his move on her because her parents will treat him as a savior.

Year of the Hare & Tortoise

Ricky doesn't understand why some Asian American males would disapprove of interracial marriage or dating, because of perceived unfair proportional disadvantages for A/A males. When a single Asian/American man sees an Asian woman dating a non-Asian male. This feeling is similar to how a straight man sees a gay men access to sex. But, dating isn't cheap. Dating is pay at the pump. A sexist belief is that a wife or girlfriend costs money. So, it may seem like Asian American men have better jobs when spending less on a social life.

The Mating Game

Single Asian American males shouldn't be upset when there are ads of Asian women looking for a marriage partner, and the ad features a White male/Asian female couple. A single Asian American male already has a matchmaker. It's called, "his parents."

The Third Wheel

An Asian male can be seen hanging around with an Asian female/White male couple. You don't see a Black male hanging around with a Black female/White male couple.

Melting Pot-heads

Diversity to an American male means, “I can date women of your race, but you can’t date women of mine.” The definition of the word “chink” to an American male is an Asian guy or an Asian woman who turned him down.

These are the same guys who think that “little brown f-ing machines” is a cultural positive.

We Are Nuclear Family

Hawaii is perceive as a tolerate state because of the high rate of interracial marriage. As a shy introvert, Ricky preferred his siblings to marry someone outside of their ethnicity. He felt that it would mean less get-togethers with the in-laws, even when they lived near each other on this small enclosed rock. There is less of an obligation for in-laws to see each other when they are of a different race. Same race marriages tend to be more a business venture between families.

Once In a Lifetime

When a white male wants to marry a daughter of an Asian father and get his blessing. This will be the only time when a white person will kiss his ass.

SPECIAL APPEARANCES BY YOUR COMMUNITY LEADER

As an American, when you hear a person with an Asian or African accent, you feel superior to that person. But when you hear an European accent, you think that person sounds like a snob.

Fear

A person's description has a racial code. I'm not saying the race of that person, but their babies are kind of mean looking.

When Father Doesn't Know Best

Who's your daddy? Is it a racist or a sexist insult? An insult to the males of a racial group, they are referred to as sex-crazed and without responsibility for their children.

A Narrow View

Conservatives think liberals sleep with minorities.

Your partner has an ethnic first name.

You want a white person for speaking, but a black person for the singing part.

You're shown a baby of the same race as you, and you think the child looks like a little you.

You can guess people's race by seeing only the backs of their heads.

You're a minority and still called white on the inside. Chances are that he is jealous because of the money you make.

You're jealous of someone of your race because he is taller than you.

You go behind people and yell, "sneak attack!" You're not American and show your plans on C.N.N.

You know the rule of not being able to lust after an actress of another race.

You're not allowed to call a woman of another race as being ugly.

You can tell the racial extraction of the person who robbed your place by the things that are stolen, and the things that are left behind.

You watch the Olympics because Europeans and Asians can win in those non-money generating sports

You want a good tan, so you can now blend in southern California.

You didn't notice that the actor who played Charlie Chan, has excessive skin around his eyes, and had a large nose.

You missed people who look like you when you can hit each other after an insulting joke. This can happen without starting a riot.

You don't mind refugees if they've crossed the Atlantic Ocean.

You're jealous when you wanted to be the token.

You don't see beggars ask people of color for money on the street, because they would kick his ass.

You don't target Jewish or Asian American kids to stay in school.

You're considered useless, because you're not good in your positive stereotype.

You're against blacks because you're afraid that they will steal your girlfriend, and you're against Asians, because you're afraid they will take your job.

You think that young white man's disease is listening to heavy metal music.

You say, "I don't speak English. I speak American."

You say, "Don't shoot until you see the white's of their eyes."

What's red, white and blue? A white guy with a T-shirt that reads, "Rap sucks!" in an inner city.

You're not black when you have tan lines.

You proposed that there will be more scoring in the N.F.L, if blacks can't play on the defensive side.

You thought by saying that your race is dying off, it would increase your chances of getting laid. But not surprisingly, it didn't work.

You can tell the local suspect's racial background just by the height and weight.

Freudian Slip

How many times does a sportscaster say "running black?"

There's a book about basketball with the title, "Only the net is white."

Casting

White people who complain when movies can't show minorities as villains. You can thank Tim McVeigh for that. A community leader would say that it's a conspiracy to eliminate acting jobs for minorities.

Ancient Astronauts

Why did E.T have blue eyes? Who's his daddy? Who's his mother?

International Marketplace

A fight happened between different cultural cuisine. You didn't consider that cooks have short tempers, so this isn't a racial issue.

Target Audience

A bank commercial might cast certain older ethnic types to subliminally target a group to put their money in their bank.

Your elderly immigrants' parents are similar to punks, because they both blast their stereos.

If there's a Buddha-head. Why isn't there a Christian-head? I'm a Christian, and I like getting A head.

You want to keep your kind in the community for a statistical lower committed crime rate.

You feel guilty when you wanted to know the name of the alleged criminal. This helps you to know the ethnicity of the perpetrator.

You're aware of the racial extraction of the fugitive on the lam from the law and have flashbacks to high school, when a person of the same race dominated you on the football field.

You want a specific racial group to spit on you. It's not the same, unless it comes with an insult.

You think pro wrestling could use more elements of racial differences.

When you're an Asian or Hispanic, you have to watch out when you moved to a manufacturing based economy city on the mainland.

He uses an obvious fake accent and say "how you say" before explaining something.

Pale Comparison

He looks like he hasn't been out in the sunlight for a long time.

Globetrotter

Should there be an African/American president? Consider the world as a bomb, and it is being juggled like a basketball. The other races would have hands of stone, and the ball will fall right off their fingertips.

Foul Trouble

The N.B.A has its terminology. But foul trouble could refer to any white center in pro basketball, instead of a player who has too many fouls in a game.

Same Smell

Our version of the, "forget about it" saying, is "no make dif."

Same Color Blood

That person is of a mixed racial background, and you think he would have beaten himself silly by now in his own ethnic cleansing.

A Positive 4 Letter Word

You fell in love with her because her nickname is of a sexual racial slang.

If you don't live up to your positive stereotype. Your marketability is lessen in the real world.

Tourist Dollar

The subtle hints between rival tourists bureaus from different countries are that they steal or kill the white-man at their country.

Suppose To Be This High Envy

You're jealous of someone of the same racial background who's taller than you.

Gas Plus

How can that smell come out of a superior race?

Big Boned

Their group of women are big. They were skinny at a younger age, but when you see the size of their mother.

Buy American

Does the American military males have to see an American prostitute instead of a foreign local one when stationed overseas?

Angry White Male

As a young man, you're a model of the tall good looking male with a bright future. Then, a higher power creates cocaine when a person makes too much money. You have so many advantages that to keep the playing field level, you will lose your hair faster and wrinkle earlier. I can't feel your pain when success doesn't happen at an earlier age when you're good looking. I'm not gay (witness a chapter in this book) but I saw a picture of a young Drew Carey. He was the typical All-American handsome young man. With all this pressure, he might go postal or join a militia during middle age.

Anthropology- Jimmy the Greek 101

Asian features are more feminine friendly of a shorter, straight hair, and a smaller bone structure. African features are masculine friendly of being taller, short hair or shaved head, and an athletic body. Europeans can go both ways of having feminine and masculine features. Sexual stereotypes focus on Asian women, African males, and Europeans have both female and male sex symbols. Do the twin test! Example: An Asian female is described as exotic, while the identical Asian male version of her is not exactly considered to be a hunk.

Adopted Favorite Son

There is a big fuss over a Cuban communist boy. But, there wouldn't be a big deal for a Chinese communist boy. He might grow up to be a communist spy. An American male wouldn't mind if it's a Chinese girl. I wonder if Woody Allen would agree to that.

Sgt. At Arms

You judge how successful a business is by how big the man of color security they have.

Come Here Rocker, Come Here Boy

Your pet dog is a racist because he smells people and then barks at the ones that aren't of his master's racial background.

Public School Secret Society

You have that uncomfortable feeling when an athlete from your hometown or of the same race is being interviewed and trying to speak with proper grammar.

_______town from Another Planet

An ethnic actor starring in a futuristic science fiction movie will still have its character with an ethnic Earth last name.

Non-sexual Star Billing

An Asian male actor can be heterosexual and still be non-threatening in a scene with a white actress.

Racial Profiling

I'm not saying what racial extraction that person is, but their men don't pay for sex and don't use a condom.

Pole Tax

American men can't keep taking the women from a third-world country. Their men will wise up and charge a sin tax (protection money) or kidnap him when he doesn't pay.

Why They Hate US!

Men from developing countries shouldn't hate us when they lose their women to us. A simple solution to this is to create a better economy for themselves. Another solution is what's good for the goose is good for the gander. They have the same chance with our American women. Well, Good Luck with that possibility!

You Have to Marry the Whole Family

Ricky had a relationship with a woman (no race mention). But she's from a stereotypical big family, so she may or may not have a hot tempered brother. One of her brothers may want to know what Ricky can do for him as the bribery for going out with his sister.

Color Bind

There are too much racial material in this book. Rev. Jesse Jackson said that everything is based on race.

So, if you disagree with too much emphasis on racial material here. I'm going to tell Rev. Jackson that you don't think racial issues are important.

THERE'S NO "I" IN LOSER

Whoops!

I rubbed your head for luck. But, there was some kind of liquid that secreted. I don't want to touch it.

Antique

You can't put the USED label on it.

Advantage

Are you the f—er, or the f—ee?

Not Appropriate

In that profession, you can't wear a walk-man or sunglasses.

Comedian

I received advice from a veteran comic about making love to your audience. Does he know that it's a 15 act? I didn't know that an unnatural act is going to take that long.

What the Smell

He thought a dirty job would be interesting. But, it turned out to be a stink one.

Friendship Games

People are your friends because you have a protractor.

Invisible Power

If everyone ignores you. You have the ability to steal things without their knowledge.

Debate Me

When he starts to lose an argument. In desperation, he will call the other person as being ugly.

Positive Image

Don’t call him fat. He’s a heavy hitter.

Mismatch

He’s only defense against better competition is to cough in their face.

Under the Table

Quickly, burn all the evidence!

Roommates

You had to live with a person who pick things up with his toes.

Nothing to Lose

He will start doing things he can get away with when he becomes legally insane.

Solicitor

Instead of a monetary donation, I'll give you my extra copy of the "Watchtower."

Public Display of Gross

You eat in your underwear!

Me Thinks

The good guys will think about it too much and become frustrated, while the bad guys will just do it.

Insult to My Existence

Is it a comment or a personal attack on me when my parents are for abortion?

Cheap

You honk the horn as a means to celebrate, instead of buying fireworks or shooting off a gun.

Complicated

The other person tries to change you. Then complains when you can't make up your mind.

Ecosystem Family

That exhibit of wildlife is not a zoo, but a place for captive animals.

Customer Is Always Right

I didn't get the real manager. They sent me an acting one.

Embarrassment

Those stores are the type where you hide from your friends. You don't want to be seen in them.

Boring

Even the mail carrier is not interested in your mail.

Natural Protection

People won't steal your things when your possessions smell so bad.

Bacteria Warfare

You put a quarantine sign on your front door to stop solicitors and burglars.

Compensation

Phonies are okay in your book when they pay you enough dollars.

Not Wanted

You can't move there. There's a hate group specifically focus on you.

Money Talks

If talk is cheap. Why are there high paying jobs that use the spoken word ability as a skill?

Criticize

You made fun of celebrities. You don't think about how much more money they make than you while working shorter hours.

Mistake

He make a "shame shame."

After Hours

A tattoo parlor is a place to go after you're drunk enough to handle pain.

Marketing

No one is interested in buying your phone number, even when you're in the right demographic.

Loud Morality

I don't want to be a preacher. I can't scold people.

Decibels of Smarts

The amount of yelling a person does is equal to how much education that person has.

Evaluation

"You don't rate," is not an answer.

Celebration

You're considered being passive aggressive when you don't gyrate excessively. Your success at something should be celebrated by directing it towards your groin area.

Proud Parents

They are happy that their kid made it so far at being a virgin, and not like other young people.

Visiting Hours

The first question that is asked of you is, "when are you leaving?"

Weakness

The vulnerable spot is you. You're the junk player. Your opponent attacks the area that you'll be specifically defending.

Community Service

I saw you working at the church. Okay, "what did you do wrong?"

Acting

You're a grownup. Do you still pretend to be sick? You're legally allowed how many sick days.

Good Luck!

You're looking for a Cinderella type of being beautiful and humble. That search will take some time.

Missed It

I'm making a comeback. In order to make a comeback, I'm trying to figure out when I had a successful venture. When did that happen?

Not In the Big Show

Didn't your wedding take place in that church? It's in a minor league church of religions. Does the records count from there when the ceremony wasn't accomplished in a major organized religion?

Crank Calls

You can make use of your boring personality when you receive obscene phone calls. You can bore the caller with how good you are.

Circumstantial Evidence

You wipe your fingerprints after touching his stuff.

Stalker

You tried to sue a celebrity for emotional stress because he wouldn't shake your hand.

Get a Life

You become all excited because the radio station that you listen to, made a new station I.D.

Underdog

You cheered for the non-favorites, except when it comes to a competition between the U.S.A and a foreign country, or a battle between men and women.

Nothing Else

I'm waiting for a Kung Fu movie which the plot doesn't involve drug dealing or some sort of revenge.

Supporting Role

He lets me hang around him because I'm not a threat to him as a talented scene stealer.

Self-conscious

Your I.Q goes in correlation to how you move on the dance floor.

Bad Luck

You stole from someone who has the skill to track you down.

Heredity

You're a mama's boy. You have the same kind of mustache to match.

Adopted

These family jewels are fake.

Men Only

A newspaper will put those ads in the sports section, so the wives won't see them.

Not Listed

My name has never appeared on someone "turn's" on list.

Shallow

Don't call me! I'll call you when you're famous.

Fashionable

You can't wait until being fat becomes the "in" style.

Something Right

I'm a perfectionist at being a loser.

Armageddon

I opened the wrong side of the milk carton.

High Standards

You won't be over-qualified for all the applications in which you have applied for these past few months.

You Are Correct, Sir!

The best man at the wedding is really the second banana.

With Your Pants Down

You're caught being a peeping tom. In your wisdom, you say that you're a burglar instead.

Visitor

I went to that country, but they pretended not to be home. I saw the curtains of this country moved.

I know that somebody's home.

Counts

I only victory that I can achieve is, when my opponent is disqualified in some way.

Can I Get a Witness

Is that considered cool when no one can see how you look?

Hang Out

Do you trust people who are constantly at the airport or at bus terminals doing some kind of commerce.

There is no entrance fee at these places.

Cheat Sheet

I thought that your ghost friend will know the future. He could help you place sporting bets.

Too Generous

That's your last will in testimony. But, you can't give away things that are not yours. You are not a politician.

Changed

In high school, I was happy that you knew my name. But now, please don't remember my name.

Challenge

You can kick me because you don't have the leg strength.

Character

If I get rid of my dandruff. I can't scratch my head. That personal quirk of mine is what I'm know for, as part of my personality.

You wear a cap. That means you can fix anything.

Gated Community

Is there a lock at the gates of Hell? You don't mind losing your keys.

Cover Charge

It's not that you can't see this. You just have to pay for the privilege.

Unplugged

The feeling you have after a morning urination release.

Covered

You put an x across his name. But, I can still make out who it is. Was it on purpose?

Illusion

I believed him because he goes to Sunday school.

Wants To Be Alone

At least, college recruits won't come after you.

Red Flag

He's single, and he pays for the Disney channel.

Look Both Ways Before

If you're alone, do you need to zip up your zipper?

Patch Substitute

Coffee will keep you up all night. You can have the same effect if you remove your eyelids.

Hitting Below Average

Can I say that I'm in a lifelong slump?

Champion

After you won an award, it must have been in a bad year of contenders.

Non-Conformist

The things you do are either a disgrace to your family, or you're head of your time.

Underground Hair-Stylist

Where do you get you public hair trimmed, complete with sideburns?

Reincarnated and It Doesn't Feel So Good

It's not my fault that I'm a loser. It's Karma, and I'm paying for the sins of my past.

Practical Joke

I put an ad in the newspaper with a too good to be true deal using my friend's name.

Lost Episode

I'm looking for the Star Trek episode where Capt. Kirk gets beat up by the local toughs, after he hits on a local woman at a local drinking establishment.

Impression

I don't know if that person could be considered a celebrity when he lives in a studio apartment. It depends on which city you live in, where there are different standards on who's considered famous.

Neighbors

I have to turn down the volume of the television during the birth scene because with only the audio, it sounds like I'm watching a porno movie to a person living next door.

Wrong Message

Angels are supposed to be pure. Why do they cast actresses to play angels for the purpose of giving you a woody?

Machismo

I'm a jerk to the what power. That means being a jerk many times over the base number of being a guy.

Happy Story

Your success story has someone else failing. That has to happen in order for you to achieve something.

Common

It's like an ass. Everybody has one.

Consolation Prize

I'm not a loser. I came in second.

Scent

I don't want to go there. He's an introvert who keeps his urine in his home for study purposes.

Sentimental

I cried while watching Forest Gump and not during Schniedler's List because I can identify with being a doofess, and not suffering mass grief.

Connection

Does drug dealing go with being involved in a tinted window auto shop?

Slow-Wit

I drink like a drunk, and eat like a fat guy!

Sibling Rivalry

I didn't want to write down the "Dr." before my younger brother's name, which upset an elder relative. How would you feel when your younger relative is more successful than you?

Future

I predict that person will be involved in a stand-off with the police.

Name Calling

My first name rhymes with a body part. Why did my parents name me Rickhead?

Introvert

I can teach, but I just don't want to be around people.

Modern Interpretation

I know there's a lot of fighting in the Bible. But, where is it written of taunting during battles, with the cry of, "you want a piece of me!"

Long Time Ago

You object to looking into your past with the claim of having statue of limitations.

Make a Difference

My only claim to existence is taking up space.

Excuse Me

Why did I do that? I got a pretend wife and kids to feed?

Modesty

I can be rich and famous too, but I don't want to be a show-off!

Humanity

I don't want to work if it takes away the livelihood of someone else doing that job.

Concept of Time

Just a minute, and you go all futuristic on me.

Mouth Mask

I don't want to be near that guy who smells like Vick's Vapor rub. I don't want to catch something from him.

Serious Expression

I can't be seen smiling because someone will be jealous as to why I'm happy.

Camouflage

You wear white BVD's to cover your public hair dandruff.

Remember the Good Old Days

The class hijackers came to your class reunion. They robbed you for all times sakes.

Concentration

Do you need to yell be quiet, I can't read the subtitles?

Lower Prices

The isolation tank you had, was of being locked in the car trunk.

Knowledge

You asked for advice from a person with no friends.

Cruelty

Why did you kill that small animal? It wasn't cute when it was biting you!

Temporary

You had someone hit you on the top of your head. These lumps will help you reach the minimum height requirement.

Model Victim

She was too shy to ask the kidnappers for anything.

Freedom of Choice

You decided which religion to belong to, by which church has the loudest sounding bell and decor.

Battle Royal

Two people with fake superpowers will challenge each other in a pier 9 brawl.

Doorman

That business might be involved in illegal activities, because their are big guys out in front of the place.

Threats

You're going to disown me! Is that a bad thing? I don't want to be own by anybody.

Ultimate Challenge

Suicide is not for the weak. You try it!

Motive

That non-profit business doesn't charge in currency, but payments are in souls!

Spokesperson

You judge that row by who sits in the aisle seat.

Car Motel Trap

You don't wash your car because you don't want thugs to sit on it.

Follow the Leader

You trust a person who says to be free of your possessions. I wonder where the possessions will end up in whose hands.

Good Phone

How can collect calls numbers be in business?

2 Card Monty

If I'm lying, I'll pay you. All right, I lied about paying you!

Window of Your Soul

What do you see when you look into my eyes? Aside from seeing a moron, what else?

Compliment

You bragged that a crack whore made a pass at you.

Free Advertisement

The caught on tape criminals just happen to have the name of your business on their shirts.

Ignorance

You committed a crime because you didn't know it's illegal to break a law.

Lifetime Career

You're a kleptomania who only steals from mean people.

Fakes

You steal things, and then pretend to return it!

Father Knows Best

Your girlfriend's father can spot a phony boyfriend.

Honored

You can wait a whole lifetime to be bought out by someone offering you big bucks.

Calming Advice

You tell a yelling person, "you sound upset."

Good Thing

You don't have the charisma to start a group of people, who will riot for you.

Time Is Money

You're mad at businesses that make you wait when you're a customer there, so when they come to your place of business. You do the same thing and waste their time.

Death Penalty

You can't be shot execution style because you contain explosive gases.

Untalented

You lost in an amateur contest with an all straight female audience, to a female stripper.

Penalty Box

You're deducted two points for hitting below the belt, one point for each testicle.

Concept of Time

You can't tell when you watch the usually viewing habits' programs. How about if it's light or dark outside, when watching those set time shows?

Waiting

I don't think I'll hear this statement aim towards me, "this is for the championship!"

V.I.P

I'm honored when you pushed people out of the way to get to me.

Prank

It's the wrong time to do the "what time is it" trick to look at his watch, when he's carrying explosives.

Members Only

The only one time I was invited to an occasion, it was for my own death.

Benefits

I wasn't fired but I was put on permanent vacation.

On the Team

You're employed there, because there might be a case where they will need a scapegoat.

Error

How many times when making a mistake, can you use the "lost it in the sun" excuse?

Caller I.D

I won't call the cable provider when a station has technical problems, because I think that they might write down my name for the embarrassing program that I'm watching.

Premature

I shouldn't say congratulations yet. I didn't say I did it yet, but I was thinking about doing it.

Analogy

Baseball is like life. No wonder, when they get you out. They pass the ball around the infield to taunt you.

Psychotic

He's not stable enough to be laughed at, you know about his condition.

High Rise

You're a teenager who doesn't live in a house. You don't have the chore of cleaning and washing the garage.

Spit or Swallow

I don't want to go to a place with a bitter aftertaste.

Posse

He is always caught on tape with his hanger-ons holding him back and saying, "no, no" when running into a confrontation with a fan. He has a short temper.

Wanted Man

I will never hear when referring to me, "do whatever it takes to sign him!"

Present Company

You made a great quote. But the place and the people around you, it took away the attention away from what was said.

Standing O

Your colleagues cheer when you go on vacation.

Insulted

You don't mind being called a "jerk-off," because it's named after a pleasurable experience.

Inspiration

You wrote the best stuff while drinking slurpees too fast, and having ice-cream headaches.

Difference

You're not stupid. You just do stupid things.

Make Way

You pretend that you're late for something, so that you can knock people over in your way.

Ignorance is Bliss

When a relative with a baby says, "I think he likes you." No wonder, he has no reference about me.

Non-Professional

I can do the same thing. I just don't get paid for it.

Infamous

Your father's day tribute is on "Cops."

Consistency

Your performance is always on an off day or an off night.

555

Nobody called you. Well, I gave the wrong number anyway!

Attention

I'll take any chant that I can get. Even those "you suck" ones.

Three Stooges

I liked the serious idiot one in the group.

Good or Bad Thing

At least, no one will steal your clothes for selling and personal use.

Move On

You bumped into someone, and he just stands there. He is supposed to keep moving.

Lethal Weapon

Don't laugh at me when I'm only armed with my brains.

Trouble

He is the leader of the mindless.

Enough Already

How many times can he say sorry? Even those that are truths about you.

Security Purposes

You trust me. Why did you want my thumbprint?

Hired

Were you cleared of all charges?

Life Experiences

There aren't much things in life you can do, that aren't demeaning in some way.

Accused

He is known for, "what, what did I do?"

Rude

You have no patience for people who answer in "huh."

Now

When will it be my time to do unto others?

Pick a Hand

You have a decision to make between the money, or the feelin' good.

Out of League

You don't even rate, while their unattractive people are still good looking.

Dictation

We didn't hear his last words, because his secretary wasn't there to write it down.

Release Form

The guy with a Mosaic face dot has his own show.

Challenge

Your rival has a feminine voice.

Stay Cool

I can't show excitement. I'm supposed to go to the next room and hide my joyful expression.

Bite Your Lip

You're not supposed to laugh at a person with a weapon in his hand at that moment.

Flattery

A salesperson can sell me anything if I'm called handsome.

Rules

There are things that a shirtless guy can't do. He can't eat food with his chest hairs getting in the way.

He can't work at the office without a shirt.

Out of the Package

You're lucky that you got it before it shrunk from the normal size.

The Truth Squad

You can be honest with me. Your response is, "okay, enough with the obscenities!"

What Kind of Business

When you made you first dollar. Did you catch anything as a result?

You don't have the top models for your product. It reflects the quality of what you're selling.

Target Audience

Who thinks a knee to the groin is funny? That movie scene probably has Whoopie Goldberg in it.

Hey Boss

That's power when you have someone to wipe your sweat.

Transfer

Character isn't contagious. You shook his hands. It doesn't mean that you'll have his moral character.

Suspicion

There is something strange about that guy. Why is he only filmed with his legs walking?

Prison Furlough

I don't think they should have that privilege. I lose most of my girlfriends with that policy.

Too Nice

It was nice of him to clean my home, but there's one problem. He didn't return my stuff.

Pacemaker

He's always refreshed because he is constantly conserving his energy.

Eye Surgery

An accused person will change from contacts to glasses when he goes on trial.

Wholesale Worker

I don't want to be known as a bargain employee.

Too Cheerful

Don't say "alrightee," when I say I have a problem.

Precaution

Your date carries little plastic bags with her, in case there's a need for keeping evidence.

Objective

I really didn't quit, but I just wanted sympathy.

Still Insulted

He didn't call you a "pussy" to question your masculinity, but he was referring to how you spit on your hands to clean yourself.

Your Hidden Past

The picture of you when you were fat and naked.

All Serious

You can't be sarcastic, and be a judge at the same time.

Warning

You can't touch that. Because that thing belongs in Hell.

Curses

"F-You," what does having intercourse have to do with what we're talking about now?

Atmosphere

It's where you say it. You can' t say, "such my d—" while in prison.

Enterprising Idea

People will want to try to eat healthy, and fried foods are tasty. Why not combine both?

Definition of Success

Which will make you feel more proud? What you do? How much you make?

A Few More Sit-ups

You don't have the stomach to tie your shirt in front.

Tale

There should be a moral at the end of the story like the show business anthem of, "I love you just the way you are."

Sunglasses at Night

The excuse he used, he was hypnotized over the phone. But, isn't he near-sighted?

The Ambush

I thought I could get away with any obnoxious behavior with a microphone in my hand.

Waiting Game

We just have to wait till the evil monster commits suicide.

Playing

You like to make appointments for no reason. Because you want to cancel at the last minute to screw up people's schedule.

Dog Gone It

He treats everyone like dogs. But, those small ones are supposed to be spoiled.

The Artist Formerly Known as

He didn't change his mind. He called an audible.

Show Me

You're not tough enough to represent evil.

Throw Out Everything

You think that you'll lose weight, when you clean your ears and nose, and cut your nails.

Creepy Long Distance Provider

I had a caller from a prison facility who said, "would you be my friend?" on randomly dialed numbers.

Too Good to Be True

They gave you free drinks and food. Unfortunately, they put knock drugs in it, so they can rob you.

In the Special Section

I'm always in the other's category.

My Time is Money

A hard day's work is not supposed be. Who are we going to sue today?

Curtain Call

The thing you wanted to do isn't as exciting, as when done in the privacy of your home.

Success

You have to watch your step, because you don't have the "nothing to lose" financial standing.

Dressed Better

You don't look good enough that the waiter will lay the bill next to you.

Swing Town

You practiced your golf swing by driving the neighbor's dog s—from your yard onto the street. Your neighbors will have to clean their own car wheels, driveway, and garage.

.

Load

The description of that guy is of him being more wide than big.

Just Grabbing

I wanted to walk, but someone just grabbed me from behind by my shirt.

Natural Order

You put it in. You take it out.

Audio Difficulties

I didn't hear what you just said. I was busy blowing my nose.

Might as Well

Is it possible to be robbed before you're going to commit suicide?

Strong Fragrance

How can a human body possibly make a towel smell like that?

Sell Yourself

Your biography is called, “Yes, I’m guilty.”

Back Handed Ego

He didn’t say that he makes more money, so he states that he pays more income tax than you.

Guest Speaker

There will be a slight delay, waiting for Miss Manners.

Oral Diarrhea

I’m an a-hole. At least I have one. You’re constipated and have s—for brains.

Needs No Protector

How often can you say about him as, “he means well?”

Never Happen

You don’t have to worry about the moron getting his revenge on you.

No Solicitor

I had a telemarketer offer me a free product, which will be installed in my place. That will mean that someone will be casing my home. So, where am I going to put the dead bodies already in there?

Size Matters

Did you enjoy looking at that? Now, you want it larger. Why do you think they call it "dork?"

Slogan

Knowledge is power. How about the people without knowledge, who beat the crap out of you?

Answer Man

I can only respond with, "how sick is that?"

Clear Record

You don't want to say in your lifetime, "you got the wrong guy."

Life's Gamble

I lost all my little junks for a chance at a bigger junk.

Self-Diagnosis

How can you have amnesia when you don't remember?

3-D

You made a pass at a person in their own world.

Real Super-Hero

I can't identify with a hero who doesn't wear a baseball cap.

Supposed Limited Supply

There are too many town fools. I thought each town only has one.

A Terrible Thing to Wasted

A half-wit is brilliant because he uses half his brain cell capacity.

Sunday School

The excuse I like to use is, “it’s not you, it’s me” on why I don’t go to church on Sunday.

Vanity Fair

You don’t have to bring your own mirror. No one used the 2 for 1 coupon deal on entrance because everyone was a narcissist in their own world.

No Apology

Sorry is not good enough, now-days.

Third Party Candidate

There’s a problem when a third person is in the mix on who’s your biological parents.

Dr. Doolittle

If you can talk to the animals. I bet there’s a lot of revenge stuff that they’re thinking of doing.

No Union Card

He wouldn't give a tip to the squeegee guy after cleaning his car window because he didn't pay any
window washer union dues.

Number One Issue

Sources show that the most important issues in most communities are jobs. Morality doesn't put food on the table. Non-moral business provides jobs in the private sector.

Non-contact Football

People are killed in a war. I thought you would just have the wind knock out of you.

Totem Pole

You criticized the hard working middle class. Aren't you too old to be doing that? You're not a teenager anymore.

Description of the Vehicle

A van was used in the abduction.

Lock of the Year

In big sports games, Ricky will bet on the city with the bigger organized crime.

I'm Outta Here

I will just leave when a person starts talking with an I'm a born again something.

Introverted People Person

Why does Ricky keep running into people he really doesn't want to see again? But whose list of people you want to see again is longer than people you don't want to meet again.

Substitute Teacher

Of all the Millenniums, this one has been the worst behaved.

Dream Job

I used to dream about being on the Liquor Commission. Those moral do-gooders wanted to take the corruption out of the position. Without the corruption, this job becomes a minimum wage job with good hours.

Announced Attendance

You still had no-shows for your free admission event.

No Idea

You think you look good while bobbing your head up and down to the beat.

Crybaby

Who wants to play with me? I keep protesting games in which I lost.

A Sure Thing

A person who states, "you think you're better than me." How often is that a true statement if you were a betting man.

The Violent Outburst Guy

He is unintentionally funny. But, you can't have him see you laughing at him.

Profile in Courage

A coward will taunt you with trash talk to "be a man" because he wants you to come alone on his home turf surrounded by his entourage. Is he saying that "being a man" is the same as being stupid?

Thinking is the Hardest Part

You try to become famous without accomplishing that feat by doing something stupid.

Focus Group

A Truman Show video star wouldn't last any boy kid to adolescent because of a low likeability factor.

Didn't Bring My Cup

Ricky will pass on any activity where there's a possibility of saying, "Ow, My Testicles!

I'm On TV

We need confrontational talk shows because I didn't know that people act like their negative stereotype.

In & Out Fashion

That statement person has nose jewelry. But from a distance, he looks like he doesn't wipe his nose.

Mean Mime Streets

No, I don't think street performers are creepy. They're the lead male character in a really bad romantic comedy movie.

No Need Fake I.D

Aren't you embarrassed when your name and age (over 20) are announced on the news when arrested at a teen night club?

This is the XFL Generation

The demographic for the XFL fan is for young males between the ages of 14 to 24. This is the same age group who shoot up schools. Will this type of experience be in their resume′ for the nomination of the greatest generation?

Small Town Tri-Cycle

His first marriage was to his childhood high school classmate. His second marriage was to a woman from the same town who was in elementary school when he was a high school senior. His third marriage is to a a woman who wasn't even born when he was in high school.

Last Words

I'm glad that I was cremated with all these gases around here.

It's a beautiful world

Roy Tokashiki

Have you ever notice while on crystal-meth?

SCARE PEOPLE

There are phobias for just about everything. Here are some of Ricky's own fears. I don't know the terms for each one. These listings could be considered as Rich Hall's sniglets in a psychology text.

Fear of Ghosts Voyeurs

Ghosts can see you at all times, even when you're using the bathroom. You would think they would believe in your right to privacy. But, you can't press charges against a dead person.

Fear of Theft

I try to scare burglars by putting voodoo things around the house. I want to put the idea in his head ofbeing jinxed for stealing property from this place.

Fear of Being Rich

An advantage of not being obscenely rich is that you have a less likely chance of being kidnapped.

There is nothing more vulnerable to a victim than being tied up in front of nothing to lose captors.

Fear of the "you think you're better than me" syndrome

Supremacists- They are the G.E.D. graduates.

Skinheads- How can you tell when one of them has wing-worm?

Molotav cocktail- It's the "Dah Bomb!"

Terrorists- They're Iraq's team on the Super-station!

Racist jokes- These are the Cliff notes of wit.

Sitcoms on the Fox channel- Those television series steals your soul.

Vice-presidents of anything- They will play dumb, until the day they take over the world.

Fear of Physical Violence

I don't want to be kick in the ass. (Straight on or soccer style) Is the "kick-ass" description, a positive?

How will the foot that does the kicking smell like?

Fear of Moving

I moved from Manoa to Kaimuki. I felt like a fish out of water. I'm so confused as to which fast food take-outs are on which side of the street, or at what shopping centers. It's an added complication when both towns have similar demographics. It is hard to differentiate between these two communities.

Fear of Gang-Bangers

I'm shakin' with fear when any morning radio show calls themselves the Breakfast Club. That 1980's movie with those brat packers didn't lessen my fear of them.

Paranoia

I become paranoid when the minister smiles at me. He must know some dirty little secret about me.

Fear of Confrontations

I can't wear a Casio watch. That is just asking to be robbed.

Fear of Confrontational Machines

I mistakenly dialed a phone number where the answering machine wanted some straight answers.

I had no idea what they wanted to know and what information I was hiding.

Fear of Friendship

When a friend threatens you with "I'm not going to be your friend, if you tell on me." This kind of ultimatum nonsense started and hopefully ended in elementary school.

Fear of Public Places

I can't eat in restaurants. People will look at me while I'm eating. I look like an animal when I look both ways before taking a bite. That's when your vulnerable and become a meal for a bigger carnivore.

Fear of Life

I can't watch the television show "Full House," or other sappy sitcoms. They make me hate life.

Fear of Explosives

I start blinking excessively and jerking back and forth when I try to start the oven's pilot light. What's the matter? A toaster oven isn't big or good enough for you.

Fear of Pressure

I start panicking when someone starts counting down, "5,4, 3,2, 1… Go!"

Fear of Being Too Humble

I respect everyone to the point of being insecure.

Fear of a Repressed Memory

I don't want to have a sudden memory of as a kid being frighten of the too friendly old guy with the Ernie of Sesame street voice.

Fear of No Need to Speed

I don't want to be riding in the death seat, also known as the passenger's seat next to the driver. You know the driver is a moron, and he is intoxicated too.

Fear of a Weapon

You know stapling boxes with a staple gun isn't hard-core enough. He will want to go to the harder stuff and staple flesh.

Fear of Exploitation Television

He won't go to those barely legal places that is a target of the vice squad during sweeps week on television.

He doesn't want to be caught on tape with a fuzzy dot on his face on live television news.

Fear of a Medical Check-up

As a kid, I have a bad childhood memory of seeing the injection doctor. His solution to every sniffle is a prick in your skin.

Fear of a Medical Emergency

I don't know how to check a person's pulse. The only way I would check if a person has normal vital signs is to go "tickle, tickle" for any reaction.

Fear of Being in a Bad Neighborhood

You can't stroll there without your hair standing on ends, and doing a lot of double takes around that area.

Fear of People Who Make Statements on Their Clothes

Can you trust the character of a person with a 1970's logo "Got Laid in Hawaii or F.B.I which reads Female Body Inspector, but another version to a juvenile mind stands for Freakin' Balls Itchy" T-shirt?

Fear of Superstition Gone Too Far

When one of your cat's litter is of a black cat. You will be constantly trying not to cross its path.

Fear of Success

Once you've succeed at one time, there is pressure to do it again. What if you were at the right place at the right time on your first lucky success?

Fear of Traffic Signs

The road signs are out to get you.

Fear of Misunderstandings

You might have the wrong idea of the sexual overtones by religious people giving you flowers.

Fear of Being Nude

I won't shower in public shelters and in a gym.

Fear of Being Ill

I will drive real fast by a hospital, so I won't catch anything from there coming downwind.

Fear of Burglary

I don't know these people. I don't want them to look at my personal stuff. Things that I'm too embarrassed to know that I have.

Fear of a Haircut

I don't want my hairdresser having an access to my hair. That person could be making a voodoo doll out of me by using my hair clippings.

Fear of Heroin

That addiction is so powerful that you even lose the fear of sticking a needle in your arm.

Fear of a Flat-lining Tone

I'm scared of the voice of the Emergency Broadcast. As a kid, your big brother will say that the siren is an alien attack.

Fear of Being Unconscious

I'm worried that when I'm in a sleeping state. Someone will use certain instruments on me.

Fear of The Secret Government

There are two men in three piece suits who are sitting in a 4 door sedan following wherever you go.

Fear of Being Watched

Is this a problem when you're an actor?

Fear of Being Radiation Man

It's not what's on television that scares me, but what will happen if I touch the edges of the television screen. Will I get the shock of my life?

Fear of Anticipating a Move

You want to see people scatter. A person who is about to vomit has that ability.

Fear of Animals

When you hassle the gorilla at the zoo. It will throw its waste at you with the velocity of a Nolan Ryan's fast-ball. I'm not taking a bean for the team.

Fear of Solicitors

I'm not passing judgment, but do you need a beer in your hand when asking for something?

Fear of the Distant Future

Scientists in the future will be studying your waste, and if by any chance it will become frozen in time. I hope D.N.A doesn't label your name on your stool sample.

Fear of a Criminal at Large

You can scare a kid to death. When you're watching the news, and there's a picture of a criminal on Crime-stoppers. You tell the kid, "I'm going to call him and tell him that you called him ugly." He will be coming after you.

Fear of Water Fountains

I don't drink from public fountains because I can taste the gum of the person who stuck it in there. Don't say that this water tastes like the double-mint twins.

Fear of Being Trapped

I don't want to go to that embarrassing place. What happens when I want to leave, and the doors won't open.

Fear of the Previous

I want a picture and health clearance card from the people who sat before me in the seats that I'll be sitting on next in movie theaters, planes, and buses.

Fear of Bad Timing

I have a fear of someone breaking into my home when I'm using the bathroom, especially a number two.

Fear of an Unstable Person

I don't want to deal with a person who when he's involved with any disagreement. He'll will have a revenge cry of, "I'll get you back when you least expect it."

Fear of S— happens

I don't want to hear myself saying, "what are you going to do to me?"

Fear of That Kind of Choice

You will have to sit by the creepy kid or the creepy adult.

Fear of Snobs

I'm scared to live in an area where the people will brow beat you.

Fear of an Old School Professional Without Up to Date Training

I went to an older dentist who doesn't have a receptionist. He might be too old school.

Fear of Can't Move

I don't know what's going to happen to me when I'm shot with a tranquilizing gun. When I wake-up, somebody is going to be sued.

Fear of the Religious Bad Guy

That guy down the street, he can't be the devil. He's kind of an idiot.

Fear of Fake Paranoia

I have a feeling that he's not checking you for wires, but he's just copping a feel.

Fear of Non-private Objects

He doesn't use anything that the public has constant accessibility.

Fear of High Tech Surveillance

I will change my routine, because I feel that someone might be watching.

Fear of an Unknown Suck

I will begin to tremble with fear when a mosquito bites me, and it comes from the bad part of town.

Fear of Prevent Defense

It's not drug abuse when you take prescriptions before any illness occurs. You're just being extra careful.

Fear of Not Having a History

Who were the ghosts for the early cavemen? They don't have a reference on who lived before them.

Fear of Getting Ahead of Yourself

I thought that I'm on top of the world. But then I realized that I'm afraid of heights.

Fear of Not Enough Rooms

They will need a sanitizing room after you used the regular bathroom.

Fear of Cliques

I don't want to be introduce to them. Later, "I told you about those guys."

Fear of Opening Your Orifice

Why is it that when you do your deep breathing exercises? There is someone close-by who has a wet coughing spell. You don't want to breathe in those flying particles.

Fear of Scary Monsters

When I see a monster, I won't say anything. So, It would be easier for me to run away when it is occupied with other people.

Fear of Deleted Brain Cells

I'm waiting for a cellular speaker phone, because I don't want to hold the phone next to my head and microwave my brains with radiation.

Fear of a Guy Who's Ready to Explode

I don't think it's a good idea to gang up on him. He is too serious and dangerous. Um guys, he's not laughing along with all of your teasing of him.

Fear of Losing a Right

I will cover my mouth when talking, in case someone can read my lips. You never know who took lip reading classes.

Fear of Too Much Information

You have an itchy, itchy ass.

IMITATION IVORY TOWER

Misinterpretation

Ricky thought the 10 Commandments were the result of an arbitration between management being God and labor being mankind.

Sentenced

Ricky thought about as an alternative to the being in isolation, is to pull weeds forever.

Backside Rumor

The 2nd Amendment is the right to bear ass! Who wants to see my hair ass trigger finger?

Opinion

Ricky felt that abortion is a matter of choice. In fact, he was discussing this issue at a nudie bar the other night with another patron, and that guy agrees with him.

P.A.C

(Personal Action Committee) Ricky belongs to a group who identify themselves with their sexual activity, which they preferred. This group is known as the blowees. It's self-explanatory. But in the big picture, their agenda is to be allowed in the military.

Outside World

Ricky is counting on there being life on Mars because he purchased a condo there. He needs to convert the property of the building from leasehold to fee simple.

Immigration

How would you like it if I took your backbreaking low paying jobs?

Sovereignty in the U.S.A

We don't need U.S currency. We have a Kinko's down the street. We can print our own money for any transactions.

Justification

You vandalized a car towing place between certain hours, which you couldn't read the hidden sign.

Motor In

It's hard for a communist to pick up chicks with his bicycle.

Kind of Expected This S—

A third party candidate is like a blind date from a classified ad.

A.T.F.

(A—.T—.Firearms.) Ricky feels that it should be your right to own a gun and not porn. Because a guy who sees too much porn, and he can't control himself with a gun.

Socialist

Why can't law be socialize? Law is supposed to be for the good of the community. Justice shouldn't be a profit motive venture.

Player-Hater

Ken Starr brought Larry Flynt into the mainstream arena. It's like when you want to be a drug dealer. You know the kind of people that you'll be dealing with in that kind of business.

Demographics

What does Bob Dole and Rap musicians have in common? They both scare people in the 25 to 44 year old marketplace.

Original Recipe

The president will have a hard time to convince me that he's a good kind of socialist such as Jesus Christ.

Private Territory

You marked your property by putting your snot on everything you own.

Long Winded

The conversation went as long as a Libertarian will share his views on any issue. The Libertarian candidate is only allowed to speak during debates with little time remaining on each issue.

Draft-Dodger

His rich father put him in a cryogenic state, until the war will be over in a few years.

Mind Control

How to get off by hypnotizing the jury?

Impostor

Ricky didn't pull over when an unmarked policeman turned on its siren, because it could be someone impersonating a police officer. That excuse only works when you're a female driver.

Cumulative

Ricky thought that by combining two poor people will add up to a middle class individual.

Politically Correct

The only person you can insult now, is a fat guy of your own race.

Love It or Leave It

You can't handle this issue democratically. So, get out!

Face For Radio

I can get away with doing offensive things, because people won't make eye contact with me.

Word From Your Sponsor

The name on the back of your company's softball team is of a corporate business. Do they need advertising on the backs of guys with beer bellies? They spend how much for television ads with the beautiful people in them.

Evolution

People were tougher before, but we have better weapons in the present with flesh piercing equalizers.

Fixed Legally

How to get re-elected? The incumbents just has to hire more workers on the payroll. Registered voters who happen to work for the government, will comprise the majority.

Idealistic

Ricky wants to save the world. Why doesn't he mind his own business?

Good Deal

Why can't food prices or the cost of living, be like those on the UNICEF boxes?

Military Spending

If the soldiers are shorter in height and lesser in weight. Can't there be a military discount on the amount spent on personnel.

Mismatch

Ricky has a "me against the world" attitude. So, what will be the point spread on that competition?

Confused

It will be judgment day! I have a feeling that there will too many opinions on that day.

Membership

Even I wouldn't join a group where I have the potential to be their leader.

Gossip Truths

Our history teacher used unauthorized biographies as factual reference texts.

Aw, Him!

Why don't people vote for the independent party candidate? It's the same guy with the long beard, who runs under that party in every election.

Responsibility

It's not your fault. The blame should be of your hands. So, we will just have to cut it off, and put those in jail.

Adjustments

When I move to a different area. There is an adjustment I have to make. Different cable systems won't have the same assigned number for the local or national stations. I have to program my own memory bank with the different channel television numbers.

Fitness

If you're overweight in a lower developed country. How fat will you be when you come to America?

It Is Written!

As God said to Jesus, "You the man!"

Hawaii's Economy

In Hawaii, we're considered to be a banana republic state. Does that mean we're located near the Gap. In Hawaii, you won't make good money, but you will have good benefits.

Patriotism

You shouldn't complain about the injure that you have. You have to take it like a real man for the good of the country.

R & R

Did you escape, or did they let you leave?

Innocent By the Stand

You didn't steal, but things were forcibly given to you.

Estimated Population

You came into this town to increase, or decrease the population.

Doctrine

To a Communist thinker, every job that you do is a form of being a glorified prostitute.

Other People's Money

Ricky doesn't mind that stadiums are named after a private business. This policy is better than those dead politicians who used tax payer's money for their memorial.

Stuck In An Era

You have to be humble during the self-centered 90's. But it's hard, because you're a holdover from the me or I decade of the 80's.

Amateur Glamour

A crystal-meth user will eventually be a media star. Unfortunately, it will be a story on your local news.

Foreign Policy

The U.S.A isn't going to be in that conflict at that foreign territory for very long, because they don't have an oil resource or good whorehouses.

Too Weird

Rapist brothers are just too strange to comprehend. I haven't seen my brother's privates, or my brothers haven't seen mine. Also, they're involved in doing sexual acts together, makes it more weird.

Background Check

You want to find out which occupations have criminal record applicants. Those jobs are usually high paying ones with duties involving little work

Ambition

You're a slacker criminal because your crime is too small time.

Versatile

Closed-caption are not only for hearing impaired people, but for people who want to watch television and listen to the radio at the same time while reading the dialog.

Atheist

They're not supposed to have a user fee on the use of God.

Jealousy

You would be angry too, if you don't make as much as drug dealers.

Me, Myself, and I

You washed your car during a water shortage.

Freedom

You trust people who say that they know their rights.

Unspoken

You have to know your appropriate obscene gestures. You have to show the middle finger when someone cuts you off, and not show your tongue signaling oral sex. This mixed signal will only confused and anger the other person, who will do something that is stupid and violent at you.

Creation or Evolution

You think that you can't become pregnant if you only have sex on Sunday, or do it standing up.

Nothing is Free

You think you're ahead when someone offers you free drugs. The last moment of reality is when you say, "I can handle it!"

Self-help

How to be stupid? Chapter 1, chapter 2 is to go back to chapter 1.

Same Smell

Democrats or Republicans have the same smell of money.

Exports

That country sends its criminals to a foreign country. Are those human resources a positive or negative amount for the host country?

Communist Bookstore

The shop is stocked with Joseph's Stalin, "The Rules" on relationships.

The Look

You have short hair. You're religious, but you can't be called a Jesus freak because the length of your hair.

Ribbon Cutting Publicity

Politicians who use the groundbreaking ceremony as a photo opportunity. Just one shovel, and they're gone to their office to do other shoveling.

Fits the Crime

You think that because you committed a feminine crime. This will make you go to a women's prison.

Buy American

Do you still buy American in a foreign whorehouse when you're stationed overseas?

Lawsuit

You sued the manufacturer of the safety protective bottle caps for physical and emotional damage.

History Lesson

A reason why the first person who landed on a foreign land wasn't killed by the occupants. He was probably a fast talker. He was the first promoter or manager.

Environmentalist

I don't want any development in this community, and if you need me. I'll be at my condo.

Algebra

The only time I used Algebra in real life, when I tried the meaning of absolute value where the negative number has the same value as the positive number. So, I'll say that I don't owe you with any purchase, but you owe me the absolute value amount. No merchant bought this concept, and called me a smart-ass.

Bureaucracy

You can't fire me. I work for the government. So intercourse you!

Scandal

When President Clinton was caught with his pants down. We should've pretend not to see any private embarrassing incidents. You don't mention anything, when you accidentally see someone you know, naked.

Pass Card

You have a "free to be mean" card, if you're a veteran, older person, rich, or handicap.

Enterprise

Protesters are supported by the sign-maker's lobby.

Political Prisoner

Why did you do that? I wanted to check if the system works.

Fund-raisers

There's a group that sells soap to save the whales, and a pancake breakfast for overeaters anonymous.

Slick

Do you trust a person who has a first name being a nickname of a street, city or state?

Stick and Stones

If words can't hurt you. How would it sound, if you add f—ing in the middle of statements?

Chic

You can tell the difference between being rich and being poor kind of thinness.

God, Jesus, then You

Your foreign policy can be refer to as, being a peacemaker or being a busybody.

For Your Own Safety

Our local politician considers potholes in the roads as a blessing. This helps in stopping drivers from speeding.

Nepotism Junior

He gave jobs to people who just happen to have the same last name as him.

Old Country

Do parents really want to go to an undeveloped mother country? They can't use the "we really had it tough" stories when they were born and raised in the U.S, compared to a poor country of their ancestors.

Finder's Keepers

If someone stabs you in the back, and leaves his knife. Does the knife become your property?

Daydream

It's every wise-ass dream to be out of order in a courtroom.

Full of Holes

That's your defense. It looks like it will be easy to penetrate.

Location, Location, Location

You don't want to confuse investors by having any money making projects close to the crime reports in the newspaper.

Let's Make a Deal

Do you want the apology, or the money?

Live Broadcast

You don't want to go to an area, where you have to read a written statement that you have been treated fair.

Charismatic

You followed orders because the leader was just so bossy.

Bulworth

He is an honest politician who when he disagrees with someone and say, “I hate you, I hate you!”

Chemical Torture

Can’t the government save money on trials, if they use a truth serum on the defendant?

Patriotism

I thought they wouldn’t beat me up, when I’m reciting the pledge of allegiance.

Alien Attack!

If the enemy lands in a bad neighborhood. Do the government say anything? Shhh…!

Action

A convention might be interesting enough, but a pipe bomb isn’t needed to have more drama.

Caution

In Hawaii, you really don’t trust a person who doesn’t have any relative here.

You Moron

A yahoo doesn’t believe that there were any wars in the past, because he didn’t see the locker room interviews of the aftermath.

Crucified

You feel that what happened to you is similar to Jesus. So, you're comparing yourself to him.

Promised Land

This area has a greener pasture, but that means there's more fertilizer in which you can step on there.

Mr. Burns, I Presumed

A calculating employer will hire the handicap to replace the striking workers. The strikers don't want to be seen hitting the physically challenged with a camera crew there.

From Parts Unknown

Live from the bunker, it's the liberal militia program.

Intelligent Life

If aliens are intelligent enough to come here. Are they smart enough to print our currency?

Power Forward

What's the saying that you can't be a racist when you don't have power. When you can speak the language of the majority. You have the possibility of power.

Conservative

They really picked the clean cut one.

Universal Marxism

When an alien attack occurs, they'll use their working class soldiers too. What happened to, "workers of the universe, unite."

Exiled

Pro wrestling has the right idea on public policy when an exiled person has to shave his head too.

Little Old Lady Down the Street

She is so moral that she sued the neighbor's pets on moral charges for dogs having pre-martial sex and mature cats having sex with underage cats.

State Ownership

It's mine. But, it's private property.

Gourmet Area

This location is supposed to be an intellectual place. That's why the prices are raised up for snob appeal.

Food Supply

Is there such a thing as overpopulation of a species, who are made for some good eating?

The Crime Dog

You can't fight crime with laughter.

Hard Spirituality

We had it tougher religion.

When Crime Pays

If you're caught committing a white collar crime. You can go on a lecture tour.

No Sense

I'm glad I wasn't born there. I can't speak the language.

Cliché

You can trust me, and you can take that to the Savings and Loan.

Substitute

We couldn't get the guy, so we got his classmate who knew him.

Budget

I can save a lot of money by just talking about it, rather than actually doing it.

The Other Half

I want to sue my conscience for emotional stress.

Not Good Enough

Even the A.C.L.U wouldn't back you up in your specific case.

I'll Call You

Jesus died for us, and all you can say is, "I owe you one, man."

Communal Invasion

But, I want to use my own private bathroom.

Censored

This is an E.R.A meeting. You're not supposed to hear the word "bitch" there.

Rapper's Delight

O.C.C.C (Oahu Community Correctional Center) O Triple C, yeah you know me.

Career Choice

It's a hard way to make a living. You taunt the police, so they can beat you up, and then you'll sue the state for brutality.

The Man

That is power when you can make authorities look away on any wrong-doings.

The Easy Leader

He is called the funny dictator because he doesn't hurt anyone.

Coolness

It would be great if we elected a man with “no name” as president.

Conflict of Interest

You don’t want to see people on welfare, and you hate a congested traffic.

Sleeping With the Enemy

They’re made of good character, but what happens when they become the enemy.

Doomsday

He’s the Anti-Christ when he says the world is going down.

Mad At Me

You will say that God is a he rather than a she. Because you rather have a feminist mad at you, instead of a redneck with a firearm.

Money Talks

Talk is not cheap. You know how much public speakers make.

Who Dat

You’re not a guest speaker. Who asked you to talk?

Super Size

You want bigger things, but what if comes in a fatter size.

Volunteer Fees

That is not an income tax, but the required payments of the percentage of your earnings.

Free Time

When you don't agree with someone. You can always picket their place of business.

Waste

You hire people who are responsible for you to have some breathing space.

Extra Careful

Do you need a safety for a fake gun?

You Come Here Often

Are you with the revolution, or are you just looting?

Bite the Hand That Free You

A convicted criminal can't say in his psychiatric analysis to the doctor. He/she couldn't make it into medical school.

Repeat Performance

When you try to state the same statement the second time around, it will sound pidgin.

Heavy Favorite

He won. But, it wasn't satisfying because he wanted to win bigger.

Peace Treaty

I don't think it was diplomatic for the winning country to put the "choke sign" at the losing opponent.

The Wall

Does that country want you, or need you? You just wanted to screw that country.

Anthem

This land is your land, this land is my land. State and Federal land (not included)

Ha! Ha!

It is funny when a public figure is scolded by an elderly lady.

Odds

You want to see a 100 guilty go free, rather than one innocent put in jail.

Protection

He must be hiding under some dam amendment!

Bureaucrat

Government is pound for pound, a journeyman fighter. There is always one there with a mediocre record.

Oral Support

A moron majority button will cost you $49.99 on the retail market.

Right Behind You

No one will go first. I thought an anarchist is supposed to be brave.

Body Language

I don't think that politicians have a real debate without the use of obscene gestures on disagreements.

I Will Follow

He took us to the promised land. Unfortunately, it's in enemy territory.

Chosen People

I live in a special place because I see a lot of special people.

What's His Name is Here

It must be important. The second banana is in attendance.

Resources

I don't want to be like him. I just want to have what's he has.

Included in the Contract

Our super-hero has an entourage of his not too talented relatives on the payroll.

In the Beginning, Well Not That Beginning

Why do men like their drinking buddies on their team? Jesus had his wine drinking disciples. So, that's why we have male bonding.

Smile

The only people who can visit the dentist are employees with a dental plan. When you're covered as a government employee, you can have a check-up twice a year. You might as well use your benefits.

Clones

Even the super-models will be living in our trailer parks and ghettoes.

Idiot Plot

I believe in censorship, but I don't know how to use the remote control.

Erected Official

That tax money is for research and development, and not the use for fornicating.

Mother Knows Best

You're for the death penalty as long as nobody gets hurt.

Take a Dive

You have rights there, but their public defenders aren't too good.

Steel Death Match

That employer will use criminals as their scabs.

Winning Without Getting Paid

Lawyers don't want to hear this from their opponent. "I'm a jailhouse lawyer." Winning a case and not being to collect is like getting the girl of your dreams, but you can't have sex.

Simple Man

He's from the old school of being humble and having a violent temper.

Assimilation

That new group will have to kiss ass to fit in the new world.

Hip, Hop, Country

The disc jockey will change speeds on the national anthem.

The Leftist Conspiracy

If Jews run the media. The television series "Chicken Soup" starring Jackie Mason must be going on its 10th year on a network.

The Shaving Cream Lobby

I thought that there's an unwritten law that you have to shave your armpits in this country.

Take Back the Night

You might as well use the secret police who's following you for your safety to walk around during nights.

This is Not America

In a foreign country, do the citizens there become angry when you and another American start talking to each other in English? They might think that you're talking about them.

Socialism is a Nice Guy

If you want socialism. You must be talking to and not dating Jesus Christ.

On the Record

You're proud of your quote. But they will check your birth certificate to see if you're too old to be in elementary school.

For Sale

In the future, public figures will be walking billboards to be honest as to who's buying them.

More Freedom

Those ideas were supposed to be in The Constitution. But they were blackened out by the Secret Service.com

How can a smaller company buy out a larger company? That happens a lot when there's a marriage.

The Bong Show

If hemp becomes legalized. You'll be able to sell your CD even when you didn't make one.

Percentage for a Syndication Deal

Family of criminals killed on television shouldn't sue the police for money. They should try to get residuals for appearing on television frequently.

The Man

You gotta fight duh power! Isn't God the highest power? I don't want to get involved, so I'll pretend to be asleep like a guy on the bus who won't give up his seat for an elderly person.

Finger Pointing

There are too many criminals on television. It doesn't change when you turn off the television, and you can see your reflection. What, too preachy!

Clueless Before Commitment

When Ricky finally tried to decide on committing to a religion. He thought that belief would cost him around two months of his salary.

Oil Salesman

He's not a good speaker. He sounds like a moron. The good news is that he doesn't have the ability to con people.

Whiplash Smile

Is it a coincidence that a person will sue a celebrity and not someone like an I.R.S agent. There should be a stipulation for a plaintiff when suing a person with money to undergo an audit for the past 5 years and to fill out a long Census form that can be checked for factual information or be subject to a penalty. But the only time a rich person gets his comeuppance is on a sitcom on television.

B.I.T.C.H., R.E.S.P.E.C.T.

She's an obnoxious speaker. They say that you have to be attractive to be on television. You go girl!.

That's What You Want to Hear

He said that he would fight for ideology is about as believable as a guy going on a blind date who cares more about personality than her physical attractiveness.

Keeping Up with the Ramseys

There's always that rural neighborhood creepy rich family that lives up on the hill.

The Cook is Always Right

Food service workers should be paid higher wages so that they're less likely to spit in your food.

The Good Old Days

The quality of education was worth more back then to the watered down version we have now, but that quality doesn't include being able to program a VCR or surf the Net.

Not N.O.W

Can she be considered a feminist when she has breast implants?

U.S.A, U.S.A (Union Says Amen)

Female flight attendants are older here in the United States. Foreign airlines in their ads on television or magazines will show younger looking flight attendants. Those lucky, I mean, Sexist pigs!

Big Brother

Strangers are thrown together to make a television show. You can have the same show with temps at a lunch break.

Where's the Middle Class

That idiot expert had a theory of why developing countries have no middle class. Because the women in those countries are either very attractive or ugly. So, the male workforce gave up when the step moving upward was too high.

False Wit Idols

People who think that they're clever by saying that God is a Black woman. That's implying that since we have an image of God as being a white male, so you state the opposite to insulate a racist coded joke.

Cut Taxes

I believe that a politician will cut taxes as much as a drug dealer will lower his prices after he got you addicted to drugs.

Loyal Customer

Those "ice" consumers, they're a one product audience.

E.O.E

Restaurants should hire the handicap to be collectors from suspicious looking patrons, who look like they might walk out on a bill without paying. These patrons can be asked to pay in advance by the handicap employees to cancel out any discrimination lawsuits against restaurants.

Who wants to be a lottery winner?

You and the government have just won a million dollars!

Voucher

Underpaid teachers will have to come from "old middle class money." That's a career where you deserve to live comfortably for the level of education achieved. A little inheritance will help you stay in that occupation.

F.B.A (Future Bureaucrats of America)

We learned in high school that when you voted for a stoner as class president as a joke. He's a no-show at meetings for after school activities that the nerdy students would have to organize and get things done.

Bill-Passed

There might be a law to eliminate the word "money." Its purpose is to stop catch phrases from using the word "money" in it.

Wisdom or Vanity

People are less likely to commit a criminal act because of maturity, or because they don't want their name and age in the crime report of the newspaper.

Stop the Violence

There will be no need for the police when local law enforcement is eliminated. Military personnel will handle the duties of protecting and serving the people. When a crime is in progress, they will use knockout gas from black helicopters to cover a designated area. Then, they will be able to pick up the unconscious suspect off the ground.

The Miracle Boy

If he's the second coming. I'm screwed. I made fun of him.

FANATIC

Who claims that God is on our side during war? Will the host country in conflict have their citizens yell "bullshit, bullshit" to the big referee in the sky, when they're losing?

Rich People

A rich man will make his wealth by either legally killing a lot of people or by destroying the environment. A rich woman will make her wealth by doing something whore-like.

Beaten to the Punch

I know that group is annoying. You have to ask them for money when you see them approaching you. They will stop coming.

America the Beautiful

We're Americans. We're not spoiled. We're just high maintenance. There's a difference.

Spin Doctors

They will send in a "what, no, no, no" guy instead of an apology.

Iran So Far Away

They called me "The Great Satan," which might be a step up from being known as "The Great Moron."

Pyramid

Who wants to be treated like a king or a queen? The king or queen job title are just a huge corporate welfare system.

21st Century

We're at the turn of the century, and all we have to show for it are aging frat boys as our presidents. It
won't be long before we hear the head of state say, "Dude, I'm the President of the United States.

If Our Founding Fathers Knew

This country doesn't have to worry over the Popular vote or the Electoral College debate in the presidential election. We should have a law that prohibits a presidential candidate who exhibits awkward "duh" pauses during his speeches. (This law would eliminate me from running for president.)

Government as a Business

It will be constantly, "Under New Management"

Directions-Rinse & Repeat

Every statement has to be cleared in this book. Should I publish this book? I'm afraid this material will tear this country apart.

www.ingramcontent.com/pod-product-compliance
Lightning Source LLC
Chambersburg PA
CBHW022243290526
45785CB00015B/158

* 9 7 8 1 4 0 3 3 7 7 1 9 7 *